Pablo Casals

Consulting Editors

Hispanics of Achievement

Pablo Casals

Hedda Garza

Chelsea House Publishers
New York   Philadelphia

CHELSEA HOUSE PUBLISHERS

Editor-in-Chief: Richard S. Papale
Managing Editor: Karyn Gullen Browne
Copy Chief: Philip Koslow
Picture Editor: Adrian G. Allen
Art Director: Nora Wertz
Manufacturing Director: Gerald Levine
Systems Manager: Lindsey Ottman
Production Coordinator: Marie Claire Cebrián-Ume

Hispanics of Achievement
Senior Editor: John W. Selfridge

Staff for PABLO CASALS
Copy Editor: Margaret Dornfeld
Designer: Robert Yaffe
Picture Researcher: Lisa Kirschner
Cover Illustration: Daniel O'Leary

3   5   7   9   8   6   4

Library of Congress Cataloging-in-Publication Data
Garza, Hedda.
    Pablo Casals/Hedda Garza.
        p. cm.—(Hispanics of achievement)
    Includes bibliographical references and index.
    Summary: Presents the life and times of the celebrated cellist who
modernized cello technique and firmly established the cello as a con-
cert instrument.
    ISBN 0-7910-1237-9
        0-7910-1264-6 (pbk.)
    1. Casals, Pablo, 1876–1973—Juvenile literature. 2. Violoncellists—
Biography—Juvenile literature. [1. Casals, Pablo, 1876–1973. 2.
Violoncellists.] I. Title. II. Series.   92-13091
ML3930.C265G37 1992   CIP
787.4'092—dc20   MN AC
[B]

Contents

Hispanics of Achievement   7

Days of Darkness   15

Pablito and the Cello   25

Labors of Love   35

Stepping-Stones to Fame   43

Cellist of the World   53

Sweet Dreams and Nightmares   67

The Darkest Days   77

The Best Years of His Life   91

Chronology   100

Further Reading   106

Index   108

Hispanics of Achievement

Joan Baez
Mexican-American folksinger

Rubén Blades
Panamanian lawyer and entertainer

Jorge Luis Borges
Argentine writer

Juan Carlos
King of Spain

Pablo Casals
Spanish cellist and conductor

Miguel de Cervantes
Spanish writer

Cesar Chavez
Mexican-American labor leader

El Cid
Spanish military leader

Roberto Clemente
Puerto Rican baseball player

Salvador Dalí
Spanish painter

Plácido Domingo
Spanish singer

Gloria Estefan
Cuban-American singer

Gabriel García Márquez
Colombian writer

Pancho Gonzales
Mexican-American tennis player

Francisco José de Goya
Spanish painter

Frida Kahlo
Mexican painter

José Martí
Cuban revolutionary and poet

Rita Moreno
Puerto Rican singer and actress

Pablo Neruda
Chilean poet and diplomat

Antonia Novello
U.S. surgeon general

Octavio Paz
Mexican poet and critic

Pablo Picasso
Spanish artist

Anthony Quinn
Mexican-American actor

Oscar de la Renta
Dominican fashion designer

Diego Rivera
Mexican painter

Linda Ronstadt
Mexican-American singer

Antonio López de Santa Anna
Mexican general and politician

George Santayana
Spanish philosopher and poet

Andrés Segovia
Spanish guitarist

Junípero Serra
Spanish missionary and explorer

Lee Trevino
Mexican-American golfer

Diego Velázquez
Spanish painter

Pancho Villa
Mexican revolutionary

CHELSEA HOUSE PUBLISHERS

INTRODUCTION

Hispanics of Achievement

Rodolfo Cardona

The Spanish language and many other elements of Spanish culture are present in the United States today and have been since the country's earliest beginnings. Some of these elements have come directly from the Iberian Peninsula, others have come indirectly by way of Mexico, the Caribbean basin, and the countries of Central and South America.

Spanish culture has influenced America in many subtle ways, and consequently many Americans remain relatively unaware of the extent of its impact. The vast majority of them recognize the influence of Spanish culture in America, but they often do not realize the great importance and long history of that influence. This is partly because Americans have tended to judge the Hispanic influence in the United States in statistical terms rather than to look closely at the ways in which individual Hispanics have profoundly affected American culture. For this reason, it is fitting that Americans obtain more than a passing acquaintance with the origins of these Spanish cultural elements and gain an understanding of how they have been woven into the fabric of American society.

It is well documented that Spanish seafarers were the first to explore and colonize many of the early territories of what is today called the United States of America. For this reason, students of geography discover Hispanic names all over the map of the United States. For instance, the Strait of Juan de Fuca was named after the Spanish explorer who first navigated the waters of the Pacific Northwest; the names of states such as Arizona (arid zone), Montana (mountain), Florida (thus named because it was reached on Easter Sunday, which in Spanish is called the feast of Pascua Florida), and California (named after a fictitious land in one of the first and probably the most popular among the Spanish novels of chivalry, *Amadis of Gaul*) are all derived from Spanish; and there are numerous mountains, rivers, canyons, towns, and cities with Spanish names throughout the United States.

Not only explorers but many other illustrious figures in Spanish history have helped define American culture. For example, the 13th-century king of Spain, Alfonso X, also known as the Learned, may be unknown to the majority of Americans, but his work on the codification of Spanish law has greatly influenced the evolution of American law, particularly in the jurisdictions of the Southwest. For this contribution a statue of him stands in the rotunda of the Capitol in Washington, D.C. Likewise, the name Diego Rivera may be unfamiliar to most Americans, but this Mexican painter influenced many American artists whose paintings, commissioned during the Great Depression and the New Deal era of the 1930s, adorn the walls of government buildings throughout the United States. In recent years the contributions of Puerto Ricans, Mexicans, Mexican Americans (Chicanos), and Cubans in American cities such as Boston, Chicago, Los Angeles, Miami, Minneapolis, New York, and San Antonio have been enormous.

The importance of the Spanish language in this vast cultural complex cannot be overstated. Spanish, after all, is second only to English as the most widely spoken of Western languages within the United States as well as in the entire world. The popularity of the Spanish language in America has a long history.

In addition to Spanish exploration of the New World, the great Spanish literary tradition served as a vehicle for bringing the language and culture to America. Interest in Spanish literature in America began when English immigrants brought with them translations of Spanish masterpieces of the Golden Age. As early as 1683, private libraries in Philadelphia and Boston contained copies of the first picaresque novel, *Lazarillo de Tormes*, translations of Francisco de Quevedo's *Los Sueños*, and copies of the immortal epic of reality and illusion *Don Quixote*, by the great Spanish writer Miguel de Cervantes. It would not be surprising if Cotton Mather, the arch-Puritan, read *Don Quixote* in its original Spanish, if only to enrich his vocabulary in preparation for his writing *La fe del cristiano en 24 artículos de la Institución de Cristo, enviada a los españoles para que abran sus ojos* (The Christian's Faith in 24 Articles of the Institution of Christ, Sent to the Spaniards to Open Their Eyes), published in Boston in 1699.

Over the years, Spanish authors and their works have had a vast influence on American literature—from Washington Irving, John Steinbeck, and Ernest Hemingway in the novel to Henry Wadsworth Longfellow and Archibald MacLeish in poetry. Such important American writers as James Fenimore Cooper, Edgar Allan Poe, Walt Whitman, Mark Twain, and Herman Melville all owe a sizable debt to the Spanish literary tradition. Some writers, such as Willa Cather and Maxwell Anderson, who explored Spanish themes they came into contact with in the American Southwest and Mexico, were influenced less directly but no less profoundly.

Important contributions to a knowledge of Spanish culture in the United States were also made by many lesser known individuals—teachers, publishers, historians, entrepreneurs, and others—with a love for Spanish culture. One of the most significant of these contributions was made by Abiel Smith, a Harvard College graduate of the class of 1764, when he bequeathed stock worth $20,000 to Harvard for the support of a professor of French and Spanish. By 1819 this endowment had produced enough income to appoint a professor, and the philologist and humanist George Ticknor became the first holder of the Abiel Smith Chair, which was the very first endowed Chair at Harvard University. Other illustrious holders of the Smith Chair would include the poets Henry Wadsworth Longfellow and James Russell Lowell.

A highly respected teacher and scholar, Ticknor was also a collector of Spanish books, and as such he made a very special contribution to America's knowledge of Spanish culture. He was instrumental in amassing for Harvard libraries one of the first and most impressive collections of Spanish books in the United States. He also had a valuable personal collection of Spanish books and manuscripts, which he bequeathed to the Boston Public Library.

With the creation of the Abiel Smith Chair, Spanish language and literature courses became part of the curriculum at Harvard, which also went on to become the first American university to offer graduate studies in Romance languages. Other colleges and universities throughout the United States gradually followed Harvard's example, and today Spanish language and culture may be studied at most American institutions of higher learning.

No discussion of the Spanish influence in the United States, however brief, would be complete without a mention of the Spanish influence on art. Important American artists such as John Singer Sargent, James A. M. Whistler, Thomas Eakins, and Mary Cassatt all explored Spanish subjects and experimented with Spanish techniques. Virtually every serious American artist living today has studied the work of the Spanish masters as well as the great 20th-century Spanish painters Salvador Dalí, Joan Miró, and Pablo Picasso.

The most pervasive Spanish influence in America, however, has probably been in music. Compositions such as Leonard Bernstein's *West Side Story*, the Latinization of William Shakespeare's *Romeo and Juliet* set in New York's Puerto Rican quarter, and Aaron Copland's *Salon Mexico* are two obvious examples. In general, one can hear the influence of Latin rhythms—from tango to mambo, from guaracha to salsa—in virtually every form of American music.

This series of biographies, which Chelsea House has published under the general title HISPANICS OF ACHIEVEMENT, constitutes further recognition of—and a renewed effort to bring forth to the consciousness of America's young people—the contributions that Hispanic people have made not only in the United States but throughout the civilized world. The men and women who are featured in this series have attained a high level of accomplishment in their respective fields of endeavor and have made a permanent mark on American society.

The title of this series must be understood in its broadest possible sense: The term *Hispanics* is intended to include Spaniards, Spanish Americans, and individuals from many countries whose language and culture have either direct or indirect Spanish origins. The names of many of the people included in this series will be immediately familiar; others will be less recognizable. All, however, have attained recognition within their own countries, and often their fame has transcended their borders.

The series HISPANICS OF ACHIEVEMENT thus addresses the attainments and struggles of Hispanic people in the United States and seeks to tell the stories of individuals whose personal and professional lives in some way reflect the larger Hispanic experience. These stories are exemplary of what human beings can accomplish, often against daunting odds and by extraordinary personal sacrifice, where there is conviction and determination. Fray Junípero Serra, the 18th-century Spanish Franciscan missionary, is one such individual. Although in very poor health, he devoted the last 15 years of his life to the foundation of missions throughout California—then a mostly unsettled expanse of land— in an effort to bring a better life to Native Americans through the cultivation of crafts and animal husbandry. An example from recent times, the Mexican-American labor leader Cesar Chavez has battled bitter opposition and made untold personal sacrifices in his effort to help poor agricultural workers who have been exploited for decades on farms throughout the Southwest.

The talent with which each one of these men and women may have been endowed required dedication and hard work to develop and become fully realized. Many of them have enjoyed rewards for their efforts during their own lifetime, whereas others have died poor and unrecognized. For some it took a long time to achieve their goals, for others success came at an early age, and for still others the struggle continues. All of them, however, stand out as people whose lives have made a difference, whose achievements we need to recognize today and should continue to honor in the future.

Pablo Casals

The renowned cellist Pablo Casals performs a Bach sonata at the United Nations in New York City on October 24, 1958, at a concert commemorating the UN's 13th anniversary. Casals was deeply committed to the struggle for world peace and often performed in support of the peace movement.

CHAPTER ONE

Days of Darkness

In the early evening hours of July 18, 1936, Pablo Casals made his way down the winding streets and through the plaza to Barcelona's Orfeo Catalan Palace of Music, one of Spain's great music halls, where his Orquesta Pau Casals would soon be rehearsing. The orchestra was scheduled to give a concert the next evening, and this would be the last rehearsal before the performance. The program was to feature Ludwig van Beethoven's Ninth Symphony, with its renowned choral finale incorporating Friedrich von Schiller's hymn to brotherhood and love, "Ode to Joy."

Five years earlier, the orchestra had performed Beethoven's Ninth for an audience of 20,000 at the Palace of Montjuich to celebrate the birth of the Spanish Republic. At the time there had been great hope for the future of Spain and peace in the world. But in subsequent years, political instability and economic hardship had dashed the hopes and dreams of many Europeans, and instead of peace and prosperity, they now faced the brutality of political oppression and the threat of war.

Casals, 59 years old and one of the world's most widely known and highly respected musicians, was devoted to his music, but not blindly so. He had turned down invitations to perform in Germany and Italy, where brutal dictators had ordered the arrest, torture, and the execution of thousands of Jews and political dissidents. Casals was outspoken about his decision not to perform in these countries. He believed that people of conscience, particularly those of international stature, had a duty to take a public stand against political oppression in all its forms, and he refused to play in countries where oppressive governments committed brutal crimes against humanity.

In Germany, the Nazi leader Adolf Hitler, in power since 1933, had whipped up a frenzy of support for his Fascist regime. He found scapegoats for Germany's economic ills and ordered the murder of thousands of labor leaders, socialists, and others who resisted his regime. The principal targets of Hitler's hate campaign were the Jews, whom the Nazis blamed for almost all of Germany's problems.

The Italian dictator, Benito Mussolini, founder and leader of the Fascist party in Italy, became that country's leader in 1922 and absolute dictator in 1925. Although he had begun his political career as a professed socialist, stressing the need for land reform and a redistribution of the nation's wealth, he soon realized that he stood to gain more personally by siding with the rich and so kept moving toward the right. Eventually he rose to power by capitalizing on the upper class's fear of a workers' revolution. He ran the country by intimidation and brutality, unleashing gangs of black-shirted thugs on the citizenry, murdering socialists, jailing striking workers, and shutting down the country's newspapers. In 1935, Mussolini began a campaign to export fascism and create his own empire. On his orders, Italian armies swept through the African country of Ethiopia, carrying out brutal massacres. The United States tried to thwart Mussolini's efforts by declaring an embargo on munitions to Italy. But the embargo was unsuccessful because

U.S. businessmen grew rich selling oil to Mussolini, enabling him to win his war abroad and to tighten his grip on Italy.

The world watched in fear as Hitler and Mussolini consolidated power and forcibly expanded their sphere of influence, but there was no concerted international effort to check the spread of fascism. There were, however, pockets of protest around the world. For example, although the Western powers agreed to participate as usual in the 1936 Olympics, to be held in Berlin, Casals and other noted Spaniards convinced the Spanish government to boycott the games to protest the political oppression in Germany. Spain scheduled an alternative event, the Barcelona Olympiad, and invited the nations of the world to send their athletes to Spain instead of Germany. To open the festivities of the Barcelona Olympiad, the Orquesta Pau Casals would play the glorious Ninth Symphony of Beethoven.

As Casals made his way toward the Palace of Music, he knew that the boycott would have little effect on the fascist movement, which was rapidly spreading through Europe. In Spain, the Falangists, a pro-Fascist group, already threatened to topple the fragile democracy.

For days Casals had listened to the radio in his San Salvador beach house, an hour's drive from Barcelona. Although the Popular Front, a prodemocracy coalition, had swept the elections in February, the Fascists had no respect for democracy. The Four Insurgent Generals, as they were called, among them Francisco Franco, who had recently led the slaughter of striking miners in Asturias, had staged a successful rebellion in the Spanish colony of Morocco in North Africa. Now they directed officers stationed in Spain to overthrow the government.

President Manuel Azaña had assured the Spanish people that the plot was confined to Morocco and that the Four Insurgent Generals, who called themselves the Nationalists, had been fired. But only the day before, July 17, refugees fleeing Seville had a far different story to tell. General Gonzalo Queipo de Llano's garrison

Citizens of Barcelona, Spain, climb over the wreckage of a building after an air raid on their city by rebel bombers in July 1936. The man who ordered the bombing, General Francisco Franco, had joined a Fascist conspiracy to overthrow the Spanish Republic, precipitating a bloody civil war.

in Seville had taken the city. Truckloads of armed pro-Fascists rode into the working-class districts, where opposition was strongest, seizing all of the men and carrying out executions in the main square. In other cities, too, some army garrisons had gone over to the Fascists, and street fights were raging. Supporters of the Republic armed themselves with rocks, bottles, sticks, and shotguns in a futile effort to defend against the rifles and grenades of the Nationalists.

Queipo de Llano, broadcasting from Seville, personally threatened Casals. "I will tell you what I will do to him if I catch him," he said. "I will put an end to his agitation. I will cut off his arms—both of them—at the elbow!"

It was difficult for Casals to believe that only six months earlier Spaniards everywhere had celebrated an election victory that they believed kept alive the prospect of lasting democracy for Spain. The First Republic had lasted only a year, collapsing two years before Casals's birth in 1876. Now the Second Republic, one in which education and the arts were flourishing, was threatened.

Under the Second Republic, Casals's home province, Catalonia, had achieved the autonomy for which it had struggled for years. For decades, the Spanish government had attempted to incorporate Catalonia into the kingdom of Spain and to impose Spanish as the official language. Now the Catalan culture and language were experiencing a rebirth.

Casals was serving on the Catalonian music council and had helped to inaugurate a comprehensive music program in the public schools. He was determined that the talent of even the poorest of the poor would be nurtured. The council established choral societies, formed orchestras, founded a conservatory of music, and offered prizes to encourage young composers.

The name Pablo Casals was known worldwide as a voice of conscience. Invited to give concerts in every major city of Europe and North America, Casals's cello was his unofficial passport. Among his many friends were famous musicians, kings and queens, peasants and workers. Streets were named after him throughout Spain. In the modern sector of Barcelona, a gracious boulevard was renamed Avenida Pau Casals. In 1934, some 200 Catalonian societies and institutions had participated in a loving homage to "Pau," Casals's Catalan name. The finale was a concert by three orchestras—his own, the Symphony Orchestra of Madrid, and the Philharmonic of Madrid. A year later, Madrid, Spain's capital city, honored him at a week-long celebration. He was inducted into the Academia de Bellas Artes de San Fernando of the Spanish Academy just three days before his 59th birthday.

Casals had helped launch a gala benefit concert to raise money for the poor of Madrid. He had brought the music of Beethoven, Bach, Brahms, and Mozart to men, women, and children regardless of whether they had money, and the people loved him for it. Usually when he walked from his car to rehearsals people greeted him. But today no one called out his name.

Anxiety had taken hold of the city. On the plaza, students, soldiers, and workers crowded around those who had radios. The

Republic was in trouble, and people were desperate to know more. Then instructions blasted from loudspeakers in the plaza: "Leave your radios on! Remain calm! Traitors are spreading wild rumors to sow fear and panic! The Republic is in control of the situation." But these words did little to comfort the many who knew better.

Casals entered the music hall, where the musicians in his orchestra were talking nervously about a possible coup. Casals wondered what would become of them if the Fascists came to power. Many of them were former students of Casals's, others had become dear friends, and he cared deeply for all of them. The answer was clear: They would be forced to flee or face death.

Casals stepped up to the podium, and the musicians readied their instruments as he lifted his baton. Hours later, satisfied with their rendition of the first three movements, Casals beckoned the choir to come on stage to sing the final inspiring chorale. In the rear of the hall, the door opened and a man rushed in, walked quickly to the podium, and handed Casals a note from his friend Minister of Culture Ventura Gassol. The note said that the July 19 concert was canceled, that Fascist troops led by General Manuel Goded were marching on Barcelona, and that Casals should send his musicians home immediately. Casals read the note to his orchestra and chorus and left the decision up to them. They could leave immediately or finish the symphony as a farewell to one another. Every musician wanted to continue.

Casals recalled that night many years later. "The orchestra played and the chorus sang as never before: 'All mankind are sworn brothers where thy gentle wings abide.' I could not see the notes because of my tears. At the end I told my dear friends . . . 'The day will come when our country is once more at peace. On that day we shall play the Ninth Symphony again.'"

After the last notes were sung, the musicians put their instruments in their cases, folded their music stands, and made their way to their homes. On the streets, the people of Barcelona were hastily building barricades.

Republican Loyalists fire from behind a barricade on a street in Madrid, Spain, in an effort to turn back Franco's troops. The Loyalists successfully repelled the rebels, but Franco's return, with the help of Germany and Italy, would eventually deal a crushing blow to the Spanish Republic.

Casals drove the 50 miles to San Salvador, arriving there exhausted at 1:00 A.M. He stayed awake most of the night listening to the radio. From Madrid there was good news. A group of officers and aviators, loyal to the government, had distributed rifles to the workers. For the first time, Casals heard the inspiring words that would become the slogan of resistance: "It is better to die on your feet than to live on your knees! *¡No pasarán!*" (They shall not pass!) What a contrast that was to the Nationalist slogan, "Long live death!"

The next morning, General Goded landed by hydroplane in Barcelona's harbor, assembled his traitorous troops, and marched them into the heart of the city. They were met by soldiers loyal to the government and the working people of Barcelona. When a soldier fell wounded or dead, a staunch Catalan would pick up his weapon and fight on. Truck drivers crashed their vehicles through the doors of enemy-occupied buildings, engaging in hand-to-hand combat to drive the hated Nationalists from their hiding places. By the evening of July 19, the streets were filled with the dead and wounded, but Barcelona was still free, and Goded had been captured. His voice came over the radio, calling for surrender.

The next day, Casals heard more heartening news. In Madrid courageous workers and students had driven the Fascists back, and two of the Four Insurgent Generals could no longer fight. José Sanjurjo had died in a plane crash and Goded was in prison, leaving only Franco and Emilio Mola. Mola had taken the northern city of Burgos, but the Republican forces were sure that they could isolate him and capture his troops. In Morocco, Franco was desperately attempting to take his Army of Africa to the mainland, but sailors loyal to the Republic had refused orders to sail.

The people had momentarily stopped the rebellion, but Casals's guarded optimism was to be short-lived. Franco would turn to Hitler and Mussolini for transport planes and receive far more help than he requested. The Western democracies would turn their

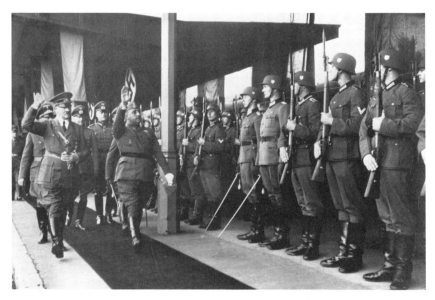

Nazi leader Adolf Hitler of Germany and Francisco Franco, Spain's Fascist dictator, review troops at the border of France and Spain in 1940. Hitler and Italy's dictator, Benito Mussolini, provided Franco with both artillery and troops for his campaign to defeat the Spanish Republic.

backs on the frightful slaughter in Spain. Casals's beloved Barcelona, the last stronghold of democracy, would eventually fall, bombed into rubble. Later Casals would remember those days as "a nightmare of unrelieved horror. The splendid achievements of the Republic were drowned in blood. . . . Hundreds of thousands . . . driven into exile. There are no scales on which to measure such human suffering."

But on that night of July 18, as Casals rehearsed his orchestra for the last time, he could not even begin to imagine the dark times ahead. His beloved home would become the romping place of armed and booted Fascists. The plaque at his birthplace in Vendrell and the street signs bearing his name would be torn down, replaced by the names of Fascist generals. Far worse, hundreds of thousands of his fellow Spaniards would be arrested, imprisoned, and tortured, if not slaughtered outright. Even greater numbers would became homeless wanderers.

All of Spain and most of Europe would fall under the yoke of tyranny. Nazi Germany and Fascist Italy would arm Franco's hordes, bomb Spanish cities, and send their own troops to fight alongside Franco's. The Western democracies would sign an agreement denying aid to the Spanish freedom fighters. Despite a government ban, more than 3,000 young Americans would leave their homes to join 40,000 others from around the world to fight and die on Spanish soil as members of the International Brigades. But it would be too little, too late.

These would be the last years Pablo Casals would make music in his native land. As the Spanish Republic crumbled, he would become an artist-in-exile, spending the next three decades speaking out for freedom in his own country and peace throughout the world. Those in high places would seldom listen to Casals's pleas, and he would never again live in his beloved Catalonia.

A child prodigy, Pablo Casals began taking piano lessons from his father at age four. A year later he was composing his own music and took his first job, singing with the church choir. He was proficient on both the piano and the violin by the time he was 10.

CHAPTER TWO

Pablito and the Cello

Pablo Casals was born on December 29, 1876, in Vendrell, a town of about 4,600 near Barcelona, Spain's second-largest city and Catalonia's capital. He was the second child of Carlos and Pilar Casals. Their firstborn, Carlos, died in infancy. Eight subsequent Casals children died at birth or in early childhood, a common event at that time in provincial Spain, where medical help was nonexistent. Casals himself was born with his umbilical cord wrapped around his neck, but fortunately the village midwife was skilled enough to save his life.

As was customary in his country, Casals was baptized with several names—Pablo Carlos Salvador Casals y Defilló. The last name, Defilló, was his mother's family name. But he would be known as Pablo or "Pau," which meant "peace" in Catalan, the language of Catalonia.

Endowed with a rare musical talent, Pablo sang before he spoke, and he composed music and played several instruments by the time he was seven. But his talent might have remained dormant if not for the nurturing of his parents.

Pablo's father, Carlos Casals, was born in 1852 in a working-class district of Barcelona. Music was always his first love. While in his teens he organized a vocal group in Barcelona, but to earn a living he repaired old pianos in a factory. His closest friend, Peret, a barber by trade but also a musician, moved to Vendrell, where he negotiated a job for Carlos repairing the church organ. Casals soon became the village organist, choirmaster, and piano teacher. With Peret, he formed a men's chorus, La Lira, as well as an orchestra that played at dances, weddings, funerals, and even under young ladies' windows on behalf of love-struck but less musical swains.

Carlos Casals was happy in Vendrell. On one side of the winding, dusty roads, gentle hills rose over the coastal plain where the town nestled. A few miles away was the fishing village of San Salvador, and early every morning he awakened to the singing of the fishermen. Nor was Vendrell isolated from the rest of Spain. Although it would have taken days in a horse-drawn cart or on muleback to reach Barcelona, the coastal line of the railroad passed close by on its way to Catalonia's capital.

The narrow, three-story house in Vendrell, Catalonia, where Pablo Casals was born on December 29, 1876. The Casals house was always filled with music: not only did Pablo and his father play music frequently, but organ music from the nearby church could be heard throughout the house as well.

Carlos Casals was a Liberal, opposing monarchy and believing strongly in representative government, free education, the separation of church and state, and the rights of working people. Along with others in Vendrell, he also favored autonomy for Catalonia, instead of the rule of the king and queen in Madrid.

Catalonia had been independent in the 13th and 14th centuries, and the stories of its former glory were well known to most Catalan children. Uniting with nearby Aragon, the entire principality became the most prosperous region in that part of the world, and Barcelona was the Mediterranean's leading trading center. But by the time Columbus discovered America in 1492, new trade routes had been developed and Catalonia had lost its importance. The Aragonese crown was taken by the Castillian branch of the royal family in 1410. When Ferdinand of Spain and Isabel of Castile married in 1474, a united Spain emerged, it gobbled up Catalonia and embarked on colonial conquests around the globe.

But agitation for Catalan autonomy increased as Catalans objected to their poverty, compulsory service in the army, and taxation without representation. Catalans were further emboldened at the end of the 18th century, when the American and French revolutions helped inspire democratic movements throughout Europe.

By 1812 the French Bourbon rulers of Spain were forced to promulgate a constitution allowing for a separate legislative body with significant powers. But King Ferdinand VII, who reigned from 1814 to 1833, refused to abide by the constitution. Spain lost most of its colonies in Latin America and Africa, managing only to hold on to Cuba, Puerto Rico, the Philippines, Morocco, and a few other places. In 1830, an aging Ferdinand restored the right of women to succeed to the throne, having in mind his infant daughter Isabella. This meant that the child's mother, María Cristina of Naples, supported by many Liberals, would be Spain's actual ruler. Men far more reactionary than Ferdinand objected, desiring to give the Roman Catholic church total control of Spain. Their choice was Ferdinand's brother Don Carlos. In 1834 they rose up in the First

In 1871, Pablo Casals's mother, Pilar Ursula Defilló y Amiguet, fled her native Puerto Rico, then under tyrannical Spanish colonial rule, with her mother and brother and settled in Vendrell. There she met and married her piano teacher, Carlos Casals.

Carlist War against supporters of the queen. For seven years the throne went back and forth between the struggling groups. The true masters of Spain were often the victorious generals. In 1843, Isabella came of age. Her reign would be called the Period of Troubles, as generals fought among themselves and went to war to retake or defend overseas colonies. Queen Isabella fled in 1868, and a temporary monarchy was put in her place.

Such were the political conditions in Spain in 1871, when Pilar Defilló, the woman who would later be Pablo Casals's mother, stepped out of a railroad coach at the Vendrell train station. Her luxuriant dark hair cascaded down her back, framing a porcelain doll complexion that had been carefully protected from the sun. Fashionably dressed and strikingly beautiful, she often attracted attention in public, but she would respond to men's stares and remarks in kind, her dark eyes sparkling with defiance. With her were her mother, Raimunda Defilló, and a younger brother.

Pilar Ursula Defilló y Amiguet was born in 1853 in Mayagüez, Puerto Rico, to successful shopkeepers Raimunda and José Defilló, both staunch Liberals who had fled Barcelona during the First Carlist War in the 1840s. Eventually they bought land and a town-house staffed with several African slaves.

Despite an abundance of creature comforts, the Defillós and their eight children were hounded by tragedy. Spain's glory days as a colonial master were drawing to a close. As resistance in the colonies stiffened, the colonial governors, terrified by the new movements for freedom, ruled with an even harsher hand. Many friends of the Defilló family were tortured and imprisoned, and Pilar's parents, like many others, were watched closely. Finally, José Defilló became deeply depressed and took his own life. Later Pilar's eldest brother did the same.

Raimunda Defilló, Pablo Casals's grandmother, decided to leave Puerto Rico with its terrible memories and visit her widowed sister Francisca Felip, who ran a tobacco shop in Vendrell. With her were her 18-year-old daughter, Pilar, and her teenage son. When Raimunda Defilló became fatally ill, Pilar's aunt took charge, carefully chaperoning her niece. Most of the Defilló money had been spent during Raimunda Defilló's long illness, but Pilar managed to continue the piano lessons she had started in Puerto Rico. Her teacher in Vendrell was Carlos Casals.

Their attraction seemed destined. Pilar was viewed with suspicion by most of the townspeople. She never engaged in gossip or small talk or behaved in the coy and silly manner prescribed for Spain's young women, and her refusal to do so was one of the very traits that attracted Carlos. Also, like Carlos Casals, Pilar Defilló

At first, Carlos Casals encouraged his young son Pablo to play music by giving him piano lessons. But later, when the boy began pursuing his dream of playing the cello professionally, his father discouraged him, arguing that a career in music was too risky because only the very best could make a living at it.

believed unflinchingly in honesty and democracy. But when Pilar's aunt Francisca found the young couple holding hands, she ended the piano lessons. Her aspirations for her lovely niece did not include marriage to a poor piano teacher afflicted with severe asthma. Aunt Francisca even came to believe that Carlos Casals was a dangerous political radical.

In 1873, the temporary monarchy could no longer control Spain, and rather than risk a revolution, the generals and wealthy class proclaimed a republic. But even a limited and controlled democracy was too much for a new generation of Carlists, who launched attacks on towns where the Liberals were in the majority. The generals, who were afraid of both the Republicans and the Carlists, restored Bourbon rule in 1874 by coronating Isabella's son, Alfonso XII. Although many people opposed the monarchy, they were tired of bloodshed and finally succumbed to Alfonso's promises of peace.

In March 1874, Carlists swept through Vendrell, and Carlos Casals took up arms with the other townspeople to defend themselves, but they were no match for the Carlists. Casals and some others fled by jumping a train to Barcelona and hiding when the train was stopped along the route. Eventually he made his way on foot at night back to Vendrell.

Although Aunt Francisca still forbade her niece to see Casals, Carlos would not give up. He and Peret stood beneath Pilar's window playing love songs until the aunt relented and allowed the piano lessons to resume. On July 16, 1874, Carlos Casals married Pilar Defilló in Vendrell's church. Pilar's aunt did not attend. A few months later they repeated the ceremony at a civil service. Pilar Casals immediately gave away most of her wardrobe. From that day forward, she wore simple black dresses free of ornamentation of any kind. She was the wife of a poor man, she explained, and had no intention of flaunting her privileged childhood.

The young couple lived in a narrow three-story dwelling near Vendrell's church. It was there that first the ill-fated Carlos and then Pablo were born. Pablo Casals's memories of childhood were filled with the wonderful sounds of singing and piano playing that rang through the parlor, where a piano was the centerpiece. On Sundays, the church filled with the sounds of the choir singing and the organ piping under the magical caress of Carlos Casals's fingers.

There was never much money in the house, but Pablo never went to bed hungry, and his parents were kind and loving. Every summer Pilar Casals took Pablo to the simple cottage of family friends on the beach at San Salvador. The ancient caretaker of the small church there taught Pablo to swim and told him exciting stories of his seafaring days. Pablo spent hours gazing at the ocean. The sound of the waves, combined with the squawking of the gulls and whistling of the wind, created music in his head.

When Pablo was two years old, his brother Arturo was born. The two boys spent hours seated near the piano, identifying the notes and singing as their father played. When Pablo turned four, his father began giving him piano lessons. He progressed so rapidly that he was given instruction in music composition as well. Pablo took his first paid job as a musician when he was five, earning 10 cents each Sunday singing second soprano in the church choir. The following year he wrote some of the music for the Christmas pageant.

When Pablo was seven, his younger brother died from spinal meningitis. Music seemed to comfort the lonely boy. Any instrument he could find, he immediately picked up and played. He advanced rapidly on the violin but gave it up when friends said that he looked like a blind musician who sometimes played in the streets of Vendrell, fiddling with his eyes closed and head tilted to one side.

Pablo switched to the church organ, longing to push the pedals and move his hands over the keyboard to create the powerful sounds that filled the church when his father played. Always short for his age, Pablo could not reach the pedals until he was nine years old. Yet in a short time he was able to substitute for his father when Carlos Casals was ill or away from home.

Pablo also learned quickly in the village school. There was plenty of time left over from his schoolwork to play games and explore Vendrell's streets with his friends. With the automobile not yet invented, horse-drawn carriages and oxcarts pulled people and cargo along Vendrell's dusty roads. The town provided a pleasant atmosphere for children growing up.

But like most boys, Pablo had his share of mishaps. When he was 10 years old, for example, he was bitten by a rabid dog. Rabies had always meant certain death for anyone who contracted the disease, but Carlos Casals had read that a scientist named Louis Pasteur had just developed an antirabies serum. He raced to Barcelona with his son, and for two days Pablo endured a series of painful injections in the hospital in the hope of being cured.

Pilar Casals waited at home, the life of her only surviving child hanging in balance. Almost every year after her marriage, there had been another pregnancy and another death. Seven babies had been born since Pablo's birth, and none survived. When Pablo was 11 and again when he was 13, the eighth and ninth Casals children would also die after their first few days. As she lost one baby after another, Pilar Casals always tried to appear strong in front of her family, but her eldest son would always remember the muffled sounds of his mother's weeping in the upstairs bedroom each time he lost a tiny brother or sister.

Once well and home from the hospital, Pablo resumed one of his favorite pastimes—listening to street musicians. In all the small towns of Spain, traveling musicians came to play in the village squares, passing their hats around for a pittance. A musical troupe called Los Tres Bemoles—The Three Flats—paraded into Vendrell, dressed in clownish garb and carrying an odd assortment of instruments. One instrument in particular excited Pablo—a broomstick with a single string attached by pegs to the bottom and top. He was rapt as the player squeezed melodies from the crude instrument, pressing the string with the fingers of one hand and plucking with the fingers of the other.

Carlos Casals, who produced handicrafts for his own pleasure in his workshop, had already fashioned a clock for his wife and a bicycle for his son. When Pablo described the strange instrument and asked his father to make one, Carlos Casals did even better. He built a single-stringed instrument from a dried gourd so that the sound would resonate in the hollowed-out chamber. The resulting tone was both louder and richer than that produced by the broomstick instrument Pablo had seen in the town square.

For weeks Pablo enthusiastically played his strange new instrument all over Vendrell. Then, when a trio came to town to perform at the local social hall, he saw and heard his first real cello. As the cellist, José García, fingered his instrument with his left hand and gracefully pulled the bow across the strings with his right, sweet, soulful tenor sounds filled the hall, and the boy was enchanted.

Pablo begged his father for a cello of his own, and although the family could scarcely afford it, Carlos Casals ordered a three-quarter size instrument from the Municipal School of Music in Barcelona, where García taught. For months little else mattered to Pablo Casals as he struggled to teach himself how to play. Somehow his mother knew that Pablo's love affair with the cello was different from the way he had felt about other instruments. He had found his future.

In the normally peaceful Casals home, arguments now sometimes surfaced. Pablo heard his mother quietly insisting that he must study in Barcelona. His father accused her of having delusions of grandeur springing from her luxurious childhood in Spain's slaveholding colony of Puerto Rico. They could not afford to house Pablo in Barcelona, let alone pay tuition, and Carlos Casals said he had other plans for his son. Musicians, he said, never made a decent living, and besides, he had arranged for Pablo to begin an apprenticeship with a carpenter once the boy reached the age of 12.

Pilar Casals refused to give in. She saw the excitement in her son's eyes when he played the cello, and his enthusiasm fueled her determination to help him follow his dream. Before Pablo's 12th birthday, the boy and his mother boarded a shabby third-class coach on the train to Barcelona.

*Just before Casals turned 12 years old, his mother brought him to
Barcelona, where he studied the cello with José García for five years.
Within a year he was playing professionally with a trio in a local café.*

CHAPTER THREE

Labors of Love

The last time Pablo Casals had been in Barcelona, at age 10, he had seen only white hospital walls and the railroad station. Now, two years later, he was enthralled by the tall buildings and crowded streets of the city that would be his home for five years. Built on a hill-dotted plain between two rivers, the busy city seemed to stretch out endlessly in every direction.

Each of Barcelona's three sections provided an entirely new world for Pablo to explore. In the Old City, ancient buildings clustered around a magnificent cathedral in the midst of narrow, winding streets and shabby buildings. In the modern sector, wide avenues ran north and south from the Plaza de Cataluña. The Diagonal, a broad, tree-lined boulevard running from east to west, was filled with horse-drawn carriages heading out to a wealthy suburb. South of the Plaza de Cataluña, most of the working people, as poor as their ancestors, lived in clusters of old villages. There seemed to be an endless number of libraries, theaters and museums, bullrings and soccer stadiums, but most of the time, the

The Plaza de Cataluña, Barcelona. While Pablo and his mother were in Barcelona, Carlos Casals remained in Vendrell but visited often. During one of his visits, Pablo's father bought him his first full-sized cello and the music for Johann Sebastian Bach's Suites for Cello Unaccompanied.

budding young cellist would be hard at work at the music school, with little time left for exploration.

While Pilar Casals returned to Vendrell to give birth to her ninth child, who died within a week, Pablo stayed with Benet and María Boixados, distant relatives of his mother. The Boixados treated Pablo like a son, understanding the loneliness of a country boy in a strange city. Benet Boixados, a carpenter, was a tender and kind man. One morning Pablo noticed a jagged scar on his arm. Benet swore him to secrecy and then told him a fascinating story.

As unlikely as it seemed, the gentle Boixados was once a one-man crime-stopper. Several times a week, after supper, he walked through the darkest and most dangerous areas of Barcelona, carrying a heavy stick, on the lookout for known criminals, thieves, housebreakers, and muggers. Sometimes he caught them in the middle of violent acts, but most of the time he confronted them as they searched for victims. Benet lectured them and confiscated their knives and pistols. The wound on his arm had been inflicted by a reluctant "convert." Pablo was impressed.

Soon after his arrival, Pablo began a five-year stint of cello lessons, the only formal cello instruction he would ever have. José

García, the cellist he had heard in Vendrell, was his teacher. García used the standard methods of the time, instructing Pablo to keep his bow arm close to his body, his elbow down and wrist high. To help him remain in this position, a book was placed under his right armpit. Pablo hated the stilted posture, and the tone it produced seemed as cramped as his arm. Alone in his room he experimented with a more natural position and convinced García that this was a better method for him. Pablo was unaware that in other parts of the world, a few cellists had come to that same conclusion and were also firm believers in freedom of motion.

Next Pablo experimented with his left hand. The standard method was to play three notes and then slide down to the next position on the cello. Pablo hated the sound of the slide, unavoidable even by the most accomplished players. Instead he extended his fingers to reach down the string to at least one more note in each position. Fortunately, García allowed his talented pupil to develop his own techniques, which revolutionized cello playing. Years later they met in Buenos Aires when Pablo Casals was world-renowned and on a Latin American tour. The two men wept and embraced. García was overcome with pride, and Casals felt deep gratitude toward the man who had taught him so much.

When Pilar Casals recovered from her most recent ordeal, she rushed back to Barcelona to take care of Pablo. They rented rooms on the third floor of a house in Old Barcelona, but it was difficult to make ends meet. Not only were there two households to maintain, but there were also tuition payments at the music school. Pilar took in sewing but that barely covered their most basic needs. On some weekends, Carlos Casals came to visit, and Pablo could sense the strain between his parents. His father had never reconciled himself to separation from his wife for Pablo's musical career, which he considered a losing battle.

Pablo worked hard to succeed, not only because he loved the cello and took his studies seriously but also because he was determined to prove himself to his father. Along with the cello lessons and hours of practice, he improved his piano playing and studied harmony, all part of his plan to become a composer. When he had been studying cello for only six months, he heard about a job playing popular tunes with a trio at the Café Tost in the suburban area of Gracia. The pay was low but it helped put food on the table. In a few months, Casals convinced the trio and Señor Tost to hold one night of classical music each week. Word of the young musician spread, and Señor Tost was pleased by the increased business. Pilar Casals frequented the café to hear her son play. By the summer of 1890, she permitted Pablo to travel with a band on horse-drawn buses, playing at weddings, funerals, and fiestas.

In 1890 another baby boy, Luis, was born to Carlos and Pilar Casals. This time the infant lived, but Pilar boarded him out to a family in Vendrell and rushed back to Pablo, much to Carlos Casals's displeasure.

After only three years of study, the young Casals was a remarkably advanced cellist. Isaac Albéniz, an accomplished pianist and once a child prodigy himself, heard about the "boy cellist" playing at the Café Tost and came to see for himself. Albéniz was so impressed that he urged Pilar Casals to bring her son to London to perform, but Pilar refused politely. She had heard about the many child prodigies who were exploited as novelties while young and then ignored after they became adults. In later years, Casals appreciated his mother's wisdom in this matter, and he always advised young students not to launch a concert career until they reached a certain level of maturity.

Although disappointed, Albéniz, who had important connections with the royal family in Madrid, offered to help the boy in whatever way he could and gave Pilar Casals a letter of recommendation. The letter was addressed to Count Guillermo de Morphy, the personal adviser to Queen María Cristina and a patron of music and musicians. Pablo's mother tucked the letter away.

On February 23, 1891, when Pablo was 15, he held his first solo concert. His stomach ached and his head hammered until he was actually up on the stage with his cello. He received his first standing ovation. He would receive thousands of standing ovations in his long career, but the stage fright never left him.

Although Carlos Casals seemed proud of his son's reputation as a cellist and the many awards and prizes Pablo won, the family arguments persisted. Trying to improve the situation by earning more money, Pablo took a better-paying job playing with a septet at the Café Pajarera, or The Bird Cage, a modern, circular building constructed mostly of glass. The wealthy people at the fancy nightclub were ill-mannered, and playing there eventually depressed the budding artist Casals.

Carlos Casals visited Barcelona almost every week, and Pablo and his father had many good times together, exploring Barcelona and attending concerts. There was one particular day that Pablo Casals never forgot. As father and son browsed in the waterfront shops, Carlos Casals bought Pablo his first full-sized cello. Then, in a pile of music books, they stumbled on a piece entitled *Suites for Cello Unaccompanied*, composed by none other than the great 18th-century German composer Johann Sebastian Bach.

When Pablo Casals showed the music book to José García, he learned that occasionally one or another concert cellist had played one of the short dance sections, but no one ever played an entire suite. Most thought that the music sounded too much like practice exercises to be suited to the concert stage. But Pablo Casals in-

The Café Pajarera, Barcelona, where during the early 1890s Casals took a job playing with a chamber group to help his mother make ends meet. His father continued to discourage him from making music his career, but the boy and his mother were adamant— Pablo was to be a great musician.

José García. When his young student brought him the music for Bach's cello suites, Professor García was skeptical and explained that few cellists had ever considered the work suitable for the concert stage. Casals thought differently, however, and spent 12 years mastering the suites.

tuitively knew that he had found great music. For 12 years, he worked on the Bach suites until he was ready to play them in public. His perfect intonation and tone and the passion of his playing gave Bach's music a distinguished place in the future repertoires of all cellists.

During Casals's fifth and final year of studies in Barcelona, the disputes between his parents grew more frequent and intense. Carlos Casals, now almost solely out of resentment, stuck to his belief that music was an unrewarding profession. He wanted his wife to come home and take care of Luis and the new baby she expected shortly, but instead he closed up the apartment in Vendrell and joined his wife and son in Barcelona, attracting a few piano students in the capital. The reunited family took an apartment near the Plaza de Cataluña, where Enrique was born.

Pablo hoped that his father would have a change of heart as his successes as a cellist mounted. He came home from a house party one evening flushed with excitement and told his parents that the renowned French composer Camille Saint-Saëns had been at the party and asked Pablo to play his cello concerto. Accompanying him at the piano, Saint-Saëns had announced that Casals's interpretation of his work had been the best he had ever heard. Pilar Casals told her husband that Pablo's cello teacher had said, "Pablo plays better than I can teach him." But none of this seemed to change Carlos Casals's mind about his son's career.

Trying to finance his future on his own, Pablo auditioned for a government scholarship. Perhaps because of Pablo's unorthodox techniques, another boy won the award. Caught between his parents in a seemingly unresolvable situation, Pablo became deeply depressed. He turned to religion but found no comfort in the organized church. He listened carefully to friends who espoused socialist ideas, but he did not believe that the many selfish and violent men in the world would permit the building of an ideal egalitarian society. He began to think of suicide, but he did not reveal his feelings to his mother for fear of distressing her. Still, somehow she sensed his unhappiness and, without any prior discussion, announced that it was time to head to Madrid to present Albéniz's letter to Count de Morphy.

Carlos Casals tried to reason with his wife, despairing at the knowledge that, with hundreds of miles between them, he would not even be able to visit the family on weekends. And what about the three-year-old Luis and infant Enrique? He absolutely refused to allow strangers to raise his two young sons. Pilar Casals remained adamant. She would take the babies with her. Pablo's talent, she said, must not be thrown away.

Pablo longed to go to Madrid, but he blamed himself for the strain between his parents. In the spring of 1893, he took his final examinations, winning prizes in both piano and music composition. Whatever prejudices the judges of cello playing had about his unorthodox techniques, their misgivings disappeared when he played. He was unanimously awarded first place in the cello competition.

Through Albéniz, an appointment was arranged with Count de Morphy. A sad-faced Carlos Casals returned to Vendrell as Pilar Casals and her 17-year-old son, heavily burdened with luggage, two babies, and a cello, climbed aboard the hot third-class coach for the overnight journey to Madrid.

*A 22-year-old Casals practices the cello in 1899, the year he performed
Édouard Lalo's Concerto in D Minor in Paris under the direction of the
French conductor Charles Lamoureux. The concert was such a success
that Casals was asked to do a repeat performance a month later.*

CHAPTER FOUR

Stepping-Stones to Fame

Accompanied by his mother and two restless little brothers, Pablo went to the townhouse of Count Guillermo de Morphy directly from the train station. They were ushered into a vast parlor filled with antiques, oil paintings, thick carpets, and a magnificent grand piano. Books and musical scores lined the walls. Despite these sumptuous surroundings, Pablo Casals felt at ease. Like his mother, he was never humbled by wealth. The count read Albéniz's yellowed letter of introduction and then studied Pablo's compositions at length.

Count de Morphy, whose ancestors had fled political persecution in Ireland, had a vast store of knowledge about art, history, literature, and music. His dream was to create a Spanish national opera. The count arranged for Pablo to play at the Royal Palace for the sister-in-law of Queen María Cristina, the Infanta Isabel. The count's servant directed Casals and his mother to where they would be staying, across the street from the palace gardens. The first floor was spacious and light, but their apartment was stuffy and cramped.

The Royal Palace, Madrid. In 1893, Casals played at the palace for Queen María Cristina and some 30 other guests, so impressing her that she offered him a small monthly stipend to help with his living expenses while he was a student.

It was one of several small apartments housing a palace porter, a shoemaker and his family, and a group of women who made cigars. Still, from their windows they could see the palace gardens, dotted with plants and statues, and Pablo instantly liked his neighbors.

When the morning of the audition arrived, there was no one to stay with Luis and Enrique, so Pilar Casals brought them to the palace. As Pablo drew his bow across the strings of his cello, a hungry baby Enrique howled for milk. Pilar Casals quickly offered the baby her breast, and Enrique quieted down. Despite the distraction, Isabel was impressed with Pablo's talent and arranged for a palace concert.

In the queen's private apartment, 30 guests listened as Pablo and three other musicians played the string quartet he had written when he was 14, several other pieces, and then a short solo.

After the concert, Pablo received a small monthly stipend from the queen, and the count took him under his wing for more than two years.

The count believed that in order to compose or interpret music a sensitive musician had to be educated in general subjects. So Casals arrived at the count's house at 9:00 every morning for three hours of art, geography, languages, math, music history, and world history. Cello lessons were suspended, but Casals spent several hours every day practicing on his own. At the Prado

With the queen's financial support, Casals was able to continue his studies in Madrid, particularly his general studies with Count Guillermo de Morphy. A musician herself, María Cristina sometimes sat at the piano and played duets with her young cello protégé.

Museum, Casals studied the great master painters—Goya, Titian, and Velázquez—and then wrote an essay interpreting each work of art. To learn about government, he sat in the spectators' gallery of the Cortes, the Spanish legislature, every week and listened to the politicians debate.

Casals later commented about the count, "He was more than my teacher, patron, and guide. He was my best friend." In a few months, Casals was calling the count "Papa." His real father, suffering from asthma and a shortage of funds, was able to visit only once in more than two years. When Casals appeared to be depressed over his splintered family, de Morphy cheered him up with funny stories.

For the musical side of Casals's education, the count sent him to the Madrid Conservatory of Music to study composition with Tomás Bretón. Casals later called the director of the conservatory, Jesús de Monasterio, "the greatest musical influence upon my life." All of Casals's musical instincts, including his emphasis on accurate intonation and emotional interpretation, were important to Monasterio. He told Casals that music was "an expression of man's dignity and nobility." One day Monasterio assembled his class to present an award from the queen regent to a student he had recommended—the Medal of the Order of Isabel la Católica. Casals, at 18, was the youngest recipient of the honor.

Many of the other conservatory students enjoyed the night life of Madrid, dressing in bohemian clothing with their long hair flowing over velvet jackets. Casals made friends but preferred to spend his time composing, studying, and playing his cello. He was frequently invited to cross the street to the palace to play for the queen at small concerts. Sometimes Queen María Cristina joined her protégé at the piano for duets. Seven-year-old Alfonso XIII preferred to play on the carpet with hundreds of toy soldiers. Sometimes Casals squatted beside him.

Two years later, Pilar Casals decided that if her son was to build a career he would have to be in the musical mecca of the world—Paris—where one well-reviewed solo appearance with a major orchestra could propel a young musician to international renown. A letter from her husband stated his steadfast opposition: "What on earth will come of this?" he wrote. "There must be hundreds of cellists in Paris." Pablo agreed with his mother, but the count, who opposed the idea, held the purse strings, so they reached a compromise: Pablo would study cello and composition at the conservatory of music in Brussels, Belgium.

Before the trip to Brussels, Pilar Casals took her three sons to Vendrell for a reunion with their father on July 20, 1895. At a town concert, Pablo played his cello to help raise funds for the town's poor, with his father accompanying on the piano. A few days later, mother and sons left for Belgium.

Brussels was the first city outside Spain that Pablo had ever seen, but what he saw did not impress him. Its buildings seemed forever in shadows, rain, fog, and bitter cold. The frail and aged conservatory director François Gevaërt greeted them kindly but told them that his health was too precarious to permit him to take on a new composition student and that they should come back in the morning to play for the cello professor, Edouard Jacobs.

In the audition room the next morning, the cello professor listened as several students took turns playing. Casals noticed that they all used the technique that he had rejected. Finally, Jacobs turned toward him and directed a barrage of sarcasm at Casals, addressing him as "The Little Spaniard." He then reeled off a long list of cello works and said, "Can you play those?" Casals, although angry to be treated so rudely, simply nodded. He had mastered every piece of music the man had mentioned. The professor continued, "It seems our young Spaniard plays everything. He must be really quite amazing." He then told Casals to play an especially complex piece. His nervousness washed away in a sea of indignation, Casals grabbed the nearest cello and played exquisitely, his fingers stretching instead of sliding, his bowing arm fluid.

The other students were stunned at the accuracy of Casals's playing and beauty of the music he made. Flabbergasted, Jacobs took Pablo to his office and promised him first prize if he stayed— "not exactly according to regulations for me to tell you this at this time," he added. It was a juicy bribe, but Casals would have none of it. "You were rude to me, Sir," he said. "You ridiculed me in front of your pupils." Then he turned and exited the room, leaving the abashed professor speechless behind his desk.

Years later, when he was internationally acclaimed, Casals was with friends in a Paris café when he recognized Jacobs seated close by. He loudly told the story of that day in Brussels, much to the delight of his companions and the dismay of the professor.

As soon as she learned what had happened, Pilar Casals packed up again. On a train bound for Paris, she and Pablo composed a letter to Count de Morphy, describing the ugly incident and informing him of their destination. A short time later, an angry letter arrived from the count. Pablito must return to Brussels, he wrote, rude professor or not, or there would be no further grant money from the queen.

True to the threat, not a cent more arrived from Madrid. Living in one of the worst slums in Paris, Pablo and his mother struggled to get by. This time there were no letters of introduction to present to would-be patrons, and neither she nor her son spoke more than a few sentences of French. Carlos Casals wrote to his wife and son repeatedly, begging them to come home.

But Pilar Casals was determined. She went out during the day and came back with armloads of sewing, working late into the night. Pablo met a Catalan acquaintance from Barcelona and was steered toward a music hall, the Folies-Marigny, where he landed a job accompanying can-can dancers on the stage. He earned a dollar a day and walked to rehearsals and performances, preferring to spend the few cents' trolley fare on a loaf of bread.

The winter of 1895 was an unusually bitter one in Paris. Coal being expensive, Pablo and his mother were unable to adequately heat their tiny apartment, and their health suffered. Carlos Casals wrote his family that times were also hard in Catalonia. With the government spending a fortune to put down revolts in the colonies, Catalans had been taxed heavily. Some of his piano students had been forced to cancel their lessons. He had no extra money to send.

Pablo was mortified when his mother cut off her beautiful long hair and sold it to a wigmaker for the rich. "It is only hair," she said cheerfully, "and hair grows back." It was something the young Casals never forgot—his mother's ability to endure hardship cheerfully. "Oh! the suffering and the wonderful way of my mother then. She was a heroine!" he exclaimed when he told friends about their time in Paris.

The hardship and frustration took its toll, and mother and son yearned to return home. They were also worried about Carlos, whose health was failing, and Pablo's tolerance for playing for tourists in a raucous dance hall had grown thin. When a letter arrived from Carlos Casals with money enclosed for their fare home, they headed for the railroad station. But Pablo vowed to return some day to conquer Paris.

After a happy reunion at Vendrell and a celebration of his 19th birthday, Pablo Casals left for Barcelona on January 2, 1896, to look for work. When Casals was offered the teaching post at the

Municipal School of Music once held by his former teacher, José García, who had moved to Argentina, he gladly accepted. He took García's private students as well.

Casals took deep pleasure in teaching and developed special methods that allowed his pupils to express their own natural talents. He also accepted a job at another music school, determined to return to Paris with money in his pockets.

In a short time, Casals moved into a house on the Plaza de Cataluña and sent for his family. No sooner had they moved in, than he received a draft notice in the mail. Knowing he would probably be shipped to Cuba or Puerto Rico to help put down freedom movements, he paid a $400 bribe out of his precious Paris fund to get an army exemption. To replenish his diminished savings, Casals set up a chamber music group with pianist Enrique Granados and violinist Mathieu Crickboom.

For the summer season of 1897, Casals was hired to play with five other musicians at a posh gambling casino in Espinho, a resort town on the coast of Portugal. Now that he was 21, his mother no longer accompanied him on distant journeys, although she wrote to a cousin that "her heart was on a string everytime he went wandering off."

Passing through Madrid en route to Espinho, Casals was reunited with Count de Morphy and the queen. The queen asked

Casals (right) studies a piece of music with the pianist Enrique Granados, with whom he and the violinist Mathieu Crickboom formed a chamber trio in 1897. Casals and Granados remained close friends until the latter's tragic death some 20 years later.

how things had gone in Paris and was disturbed when Casals described the terrible months there. After he performed at a palace recital, the queen presented him with a sapphire from her bracelet. Later he mounted it in his bow, always there to remind him of his "second mother."

In Espinho, Casals kept a lighter schedule than usual, taking regular opportunities to relax in the sun. In addition to his work playing with the group at the casino, he soloed once a week in the café adjoining the gaming tables. Once the word spread about his extraordinary talent, he was invited to perform for King Carlos I and Queen Amelia of Portugal.

On the way back to Barcelona, Casals stopped in Madrid and gave his first solo concert, playing Édouard Lalo's Concerto in D Minor with the Madrid Symphony Orchestra. He received little more than a polite reception, the Spaniards preferring the stylized mannerisms of the Brussels school to Casals's more personal approach to the music. Before he left, Queen María Cristina presented him with a cello and his second decoration—the Order of Carlos III, an unusual honor for a 20-year-old supporter of republicanism.

In 1899, Emma Nevada, a singer who had debuted at the London Opera in her teens and then gone on to sing at La Scala, had been impressed when she heard Casals play at Espinho, and she invited him to visit her at her home near Paris. Nevada took Casals to London and helped arrange for his London debut. He played the Saint-Saën's cello concerto at the glass exposition building, the Crystal Palace, and then played at Queen Victoria's summer house. Queen María Cristina told him later that Victoria had sent her a telegram describing Casals's playing as "delightful."

Anticipating his return to Paris, Casals asked Count de Morphy to provide him with a letter of introduction to Charles Lamoureux, the most acclaimed conductor in the French capital, who headed a world-renowned orchestra that bore his name. Casals showed up at Lamoureux's address and was ushered into a library. Lamoureux was gravely ill, and every joint in his body was locked with

Casals auditioned for the aging and ill but still active French conductor Charles Lamoureux in the latter's chambers in 1899. When he heard the young cellist play, Lamoureux, with tears in his eyes, looked at Casals and said, "You are one of the elect."

rheumatism. Still, he was hard at work marking the score of *Tristan and Isolde,* the opera he would conduct in a few days, when Casals entered his chambers.

When Lamoureux read Count de Morphy's letter, he blurted out, "Everyone thinks to discover genius." Nevertheless he instructed Casals to return with his cello the next day, and in the morning Casals and his accompanist Ernest Walker appeared as scheduled. Lamoureux kept working as they played the Lalo concerto. Suddenly, he stopped writing and turned to Casals with tears in his eyes. "You are one of the elect," he said, and immediately offered Casals a solo appearance.

Casals performed the Lalo concerto before a packed house with Lamoureux's orchestra on November 12, 1899, and was asked to return in December. The notices were excellent. When he tried to contact de Morphy to share his good fortune, he was shocked to learn that the count had died a few weeks earlier. Saddened, Casals left Paris for Madrid and arrived home on December 22, 1899, in time to spend his birthday and the turn of the century with the people he loved most in the world. He did not hear until weeks later that Lamoureux, a man so crucial to his continued success, had died the day before he left Paris.

Casals practices in Holland in 1907. Often during his visits to Holland, the cellist would stay with the composer Julius Röntgen and his family. Röntgen, who had been a close friend of Johannes Brahms, loved to tell stories about the great maestro.

CHAPTER FIVE

Cellist of the World

Casals returned to Paris knowing that there would be very few opportunities in his homeland. In 1898 a defeated Spain had lost Cuba, Puerto Rico, Guam, and the Philippines to the United States, and without the wealth generated by its former colonies, the Spanish economy faltered. In Casals's beloved Catalonia, the anarchists, believers in communal local democracy, gained the support of an impoverished population. Casals worried about the future of his country as well as his own prospects. With Lamoureux dead, he feared that he was perhaps too old, at 23, to embark on a concert career. He checked into an inexpensive hotel in Montmartre, trying to make his money last as long as possible.

Right after his debut, Casals had been courted by the wealthy and somewhat bored men and women who desperately wanted to surround themselves with interesting companions. It was a common practice for the wealthy class to seek out and invite prominent artists, writers, and musicians into their homes. At these so-called salons, guests were wined and dined by adoring hostesses and hosts who hung on their every word, and an artist's career could be helped tremendously by the patronage of such well-heeled fans. One of these patrons, a British woman named Matilda Ram, heard that Casals was ill in his cold room in Montmartre and came to rescue him. She brought him back to her home, and he stayed there for several months.

At the salons, Casals met others who would figure prominently in his career. These included Harold Bauer, a brilliant pianist, who would tour with him for 20 years, and Mathilde Marchesi, for 50 years a renowned voice instructor, who invited Casals to accompany her students at a gala concert. At the political salon of Aline and Paul Ménard-Dorian, Casals met socialists, atheists, and supporters of republicanism, like himself. On one of those evenings he met Colonel Georges Picquart, a key figure in a major scandal of the day—the Dreyfus affair.

While Casals was studying in Madrid, Alfred Dreyfus, a young Jewish captain in the French army, had been accused of spying for the Germans and sentenced to life imprisonment on Devil's Island, off the coast of South America. Picquart, then a major, had un-

A January 1895 cover of Le Petit Journal *depicts Alfred Dreyfus, a Jewish captain in the French army, in his prison cell. After Dreyfus was convicted of treason, it was revealed that he had been framed by the French army, which had tried to protect several high-ranking officers by exploiting French anti-Semitism and using Dreyfus as a scapegoat.*

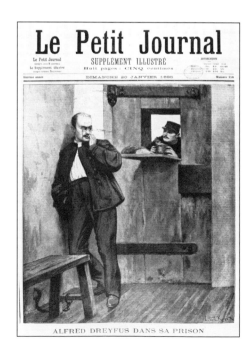

earthed evidence that cleared Dreyfus but implicated certain high-ranking army personnel. When he presented the evidence to a superior officer, Picquart was shipped off to Tunisia and warned not to reveal what he knew. But before he left, Picquart gave a courageous lawyer the information in a sealed envelope. When the facts leaked out, the government was forced to make the matter public, and Picquart was briefly imprisoned for endangering national security.

In 1899, the prominent French novelist Émile Zola sent an open letter, *"J'accuse!"* (I Accuse), to the newspapers, exposing the truth about both the crime and the cover-up, and at a new trial the army again found Dreyfus guilty but reduced his sentence. Continued public pressure eventually forced the government to pardon Dreyfus, but his supporters demanded full exoneration. The Dreyfus affair tore France into warring factions. Casals was shocked at the pervasiveness of anti-Semitism—hatred of Jews—in France.

The Dreyfus affair made a lasting impression on Casals. "I found it almost unbelievable that in Paris—with all its culture and its noble traditions of the rights of man . . . anti-Semitism could spread like a foul plague. What words indeed are there to describe this disease, which would later infect a whole nation and rationalize the massacre of millions of men, women, and children on the grounds that 'Jewish blood' flowed in their veins? . . . The very idea of hating Jews is incomprehensible to me. My own life has been so enriched by tender associations with Jewish fellow artists and friends."

Casals sought to fill his concert schedule. He rehearsed with his pianist friend Harold Bauer, and they scheduled a few joint appearances in Spain and Portugal. The two men had much in common—love of music, books, and even tennis. The tour was the start of an enduring friendship but only a modest financial success. Then Emma Nevada invited Casals to join her and her husband on a tour of the United States, and Casals jumped at the chance. She, her husband, the pianist León Moreau, and Casals arrived in New York on November 16, 1901, and headed for Massachusetts for their first concerts.

Casals received only lukewarm notices. American audiences had come to be entertained by a flamboyant young Spanish virtuoso and had expected him to put on a show. But Casals refused to grandstand and always treated the music with the respect a great masterpiece deserved.

Traveling in the United States, Casals saw that much of what he had heard about the so-called land of opportunity was a hollow myth. Although a handful of bankers and industrialists were prospering, particularly on the labors of newly arrived immigrants, Casals saw that far greater numbers throughout the United States were struggling to survive from day to day, their misery sharply contrasting with the lives of those who financed businesses and owned factories.

Casals felt much closer to the world's working people than to the wealthy patrons he met in the salons and concert halls, and wherever he went he set aside time to visit working-class neighborhoods. In Wilkes-Barre, Pennsylvania, for example, he and León Moreau spent their time between concerts mingling with local people, many of whom worked in the region's coal mines. Some concertgoers were amused and others puzzled when, having gone down into a coal mine that afternoon, the musicians arrived at the concert hall with coal dust on their faces. In the Southwest, Casals and Moreau played cards with cowboy gamblers and explored the Arizona desert.

Casals enjoyed touring but quickly tired of the repetitious packing of rumpled clothing and hopping from one concert hall to the next. Performing was important and gratifying for him in many respects, but sometimes he felt burdened by the difficult demands of the road. Also, he was still bothered by stage fright. So when the tour ended in San Francisco, Casals was to some degree relieved.

Eager to see some of the area's natural beauty, Casals joined a group climbing Mount Tamalpais, overlooking San Francisco Bay. During the descent, a large rock was dislodged and sent plummeting toward Casals. Someone alerted him, and he ducked, but the rock hit and damaged his left hand. Fortunately the hand healed, and Casals's playing was not effected.

Two months later, in the late spring of 1902, Casals sailed home for a reunion with his family and then traveled to Portugal to earn some money after his long layoff. In the fall he toured Spain again with Bauer, visiting Queen María Cristina. Alfonso XIII was declared of age that year and ruled as a constitutional monarch through a succession of governments.

Casals was now known to some degree throughout Europe. In 1902 he performed Bach's cello suites in public for the first time, creating a stir in musical circles, and invitations to perform poured in from around the world. Along with appearances in several European countries, Casals and Bauer toured South America in 1903. Early the following year, Casals returned to the United States, this time as an internationally acclaimed artist. The highlight of the trip was an invitation from the wife of U.S. president Theodore Roosevelt to play at one of her exclusive musical evenings in the East Room of the White House on January 15 before 400 hand-picked guests.

With little time to rest, Casals returned to Paris before beginning a second South American tour with Bauer. He moved out of the boardinghouse he had been living in and rented a modest house in a Paris development called Villa Molitor. He enjoyed having a home where he could rest between tours, but often he was swamped with visitors and had to slip away for solitary walks.

When he traveled in Europe, Casals usually met up with one or two close friends in each city. In Amsterdam, Holland, he often stayed with composer Julius Röntgen, his wife, and six children. Röntgen had been a personal friend of Johannes Brahms and loved to tell stories about the composer. Later, in Belgium, Casals became close with Queen Elisabeth and the violinist Eugène Ysaÿe.

As Casals dashed from one city to another to give concert after concert, he began to worry about his father's failing health. When doctors advised Carlos Casals to move to the country, Casals bought him a cottage in the mountain village of Bonastre, close to Vendrell. Pilar Casals and her two younger sons divided their time between Barcelona, Bonastre, and the San Salvador beach. At his mother's urging, Casals bought a strip of land at the end of the beach, planning to build a permanent home of his own someday, and raced off on yet another whirlwind tour, this time to perform in Moscow, even though he knew Russia was in turmoil.

Just as Spain had fought to hold on to its colonies at the turn of the century, so Russia fought the Japanese in 1904 over Asian colonies. Defeated, the exhausted and angry Russian soldiers returned home and joined the suffering urban workers to demand an eight-hour workday and a minimum wage. On January 22, 1905, the czar's troops opened fire on a quarter million peaceful demonstrators in St. Petersburg. Finally, fearful that he would be thrown out of power, the czar proclaimed a constitution on October 13.

When Casals traveled from Berlin to Moscow in early November 1905, his train was stopped en route, and he was informed that a railroad strike was in progress. A general offered to bring Casals as far as St. Petersburg on his private train. Casals had no choice but to accept. At least he had an acquaintance in that city—the Russian pianist and conductor Alexander Siloti.

Siloti had booked the Belgian virtuoso Eugène Ysaÿe to play under his baton at a concert in a few days, but Ysaÿe was stranded in Warsaw, Poland. On the night of the concert, the splendidly coiffured audience paraded into the Hall of Nobles, bedccked in jewels, furs, formal suits, and dress uniforms. As the tall, slender Siloti came on stage to announce the program change, a man no taller than the cello he carried walked behind Siloti dressed in a

In 1905, Casals, the French violinist Jacques Thibaud, and the Swiss pianist Alfred Cortot (left to right) formed what critics praised as the greatest chamber music trio of the 20th century. The following year, the three musicians founded a music school in Paris, the École Normale de Musique.

modest suit. Casals's luggage had never made it to St. Petersburg. A discernible titter ran through the hall, but at the end of the first movement of the Saint-Saëns cello concerto, the audience was standing and applauding wildly. After the concert, one critic raved that "the large tone, the purity of sound, the intelligent phrasing, and the vivacity—all have been united in this artist for our wonderment."

Except when he played trios and quartets with other musicians, Casals was still hounded by stage fright. When he returned from Russia in 1905, he joined the Swiss pianist Alfred Cortot and the French violinist Jacques Thibaud to form what astute critics deemed the finest chamber music trio of the 20th century.

Success did not seem to change Casals. He remained courteous, kind, and interested in others. He was especially interested in less fortunate musicians, whose plight he understood well from firsthand experience. Emanuel Moór was one such musician. Moór was a brilliant composer, but he was unhappy, and he had a way of antagonizing others. Despite Moór's irritating traits, Casals believed that his music was a treasure for the world, and he publicized it by playing Moór's cello pieces at many of his concerts. Casals was also acutely aware of the plight of working musicians, who were for the most part grossly underpaid and exploited by concert promoters. Casals took a stand on this issue in Brussels, where the concertgoing public was permitted to buy tickets to attend rehearsals. Concert hall managers raked in considerable sums from this practice, but the players opposed the intrusion on their privacy and also received no extra pay for these public rehearsals, which in effect were additional performances. At one such rehearsal, Casals refused to run through his Bach cello suite solo. Because the orchestra was not involved, he insisted, no rehearsal was necessary. The conductor demanded that he play, but Casals made it clear in front of the impatient audience that he was not getting paid to play the suite twice. Because of Casals's stature, the conductor relented. Casals had initiated a new policy that became the norm for many orchestras.

In 1906, Casals, Thibaud, and Cortot opened a new music school in Paris, the École Normale de Musique. No matter how busy he was, Casals encouraged the development of new young talent. Auditions were held each spring and more applications rolled in than he could handle. Casals organized master classes for advanced students, and many of the world's most prominent cellists passed through the École's doors or took private lessons from Casals at San Salvador during the summer. Later, in New York City, Lieff Rosanoff, who had attended Casals's master classes, taught poor students at the Third Street Music Settlement School on Manhattan's Lower East Side. Like his teacher, Rosanoff used Bach, Saint-Saëns, and David Popper pieces for his beginning students, instead of the usual scales and exercise books.

When Casals found a youngster with a special spark, he made the student his personal protégé. One such student was Guilhermina Suggia, a Portuguese cellist, who had played in public at the age of seven after a few lessons from her cellist father, Augusto Suggia. In 1906, at 17, she had made her solo debut. When Casals

learned that Suggia's father had died and that there was no money
for the talented girl to continue her studies, he brought her to his
Paris house, placing her in the care of a housekeeper. When Casals
periodically returned from his tours, he gave her intensive cello
lessons. Suggia played beautifully and before long developed a
crush on her teacher.

Casals and Suggia had little in common except music, but
Casals was flattered and a bit lonely. He proposed marriage to her,
but Suggia said she was not ready for domestic life.

In the fall of 1908, just before a concert in Basel, Switzerland,
Casals had a feeling that something terrible was happening to
his father. Right after his last encore, he rushed to Vendrell and
learned that his father had died at just about the time that Casals
had his premonition. Carlos Casals was buried near the Vendrell
church where he had played the organ. Casals spoke at the funeral,
paying homage to the man who had introduced him to the wonders
of music.

In 1910, Casals decided that he was finally ready to play in
Vienna. Somewhat awed by the city's musical heritage, he had
always turned down invitations to play in the city where Beethoven

*Casals (right) poses in New York in
1918 with the Austrian violinist
Fritz Kreisler (left), pianist Harold
Bauer, and conductor Walter Dam-
rosch (seated, center), a few of the
brilliant musicians with whom he
performed during his long concert
career.*

and Brahms had lived and worked. When he arrived at his hotel, Casals heard a porter whistling a theme from Brahms and learned that the man was a member of a workers' musical society. An idea was planted in Casals's head that would germinate years later.

The night of the concert arrived, filling Casals with terror. To make matters worse, when he walked onto the stage and picked up his bow, twirling it to relax his wrist as he often did, the bow flew from his hand like a bat over the heads of the audience. No one laughed. Instead they gravely passed the bow back to him. When Casals finished playing, there were wild cheers. After that night, Vienna was on Casals's regular itinerary.

During the next three years, Casals led the life of a celebrity, touring with Bauer and playing duets with renowned violinists such as Eugène Ysaÿe and the Austrian virtuoso Fritz Kreisler, zigzagging between Budapest, Paris, and Vienna, as well as the major cities of Russia. Everywhere he went he was awarded honorary degrees and prizes. These included the Beethoven Gold Medal of the Philharmonic Society of London.

Meanwhile, the Casals family was going through a difficult period. Luis Casals had followed in his brother Pablo's footsteps and paid a bribe to keep out of the army. Now Enrique was called, and that road was no longer open. Pilar Casals, who had been supervising the construction of a family beach house, was determined that none of her sons would kill or be killed by other innocent boys while sons of the privileged class remained safely at home. She asked Pablo to purchase a ticket to South America for his youngest brother, and they tearfully saw him off.

In October 1909, Casals and Suggia had met Donald Francis Tovey, a tall, attractive pianist and composer in his early thirties. Like Suggia, he was temperamental and unpredictable, but Casals thought his music was extraordinary, and Suggia seemed to enjoy the spirited Tovey's company. During the summer of 1912 at Villa Casals, as the newly built beach house was called, Donald Tovey arrived and proceeded to dominate the other guests by the sheer force of his abrasive personality. A quarrel between Casals and Tovey erupted, and Tovey stormed off with Suggia in tow. Details are uncertain, but after the summer of 1912, she and Casals were no longer together.

The following year, after Casals performed in Berlin, the American mezzo-soprano Susan Metcalfe came backstage to congratulate him. They had met casually when they appeared on the same program in New York some years before, and a few letters had passed between them. Metcalfe asked for help in building a repertoire of Spanish songs, and Casals offered his services. As they worked together on the music, a romance developed swiftly, and they were married on April 4, 1914, in a courthouse in New Rochelle, New York, where Metcalfe had taken up residence.

As with Suggia, Casals had little in common with his wife other than music. Metcalfe had always been part of high society in the United States and was not interested in the problems of working people, whereas Casals came from and identified with humble folk. Professional jealousy also entered the equation. Trying to promote Metcalfe's singing career, Casals often accompanied her on the piano at her concerts. The reviewers raved about the cellist's ability as a piano accompanist, whereas the reviews of Metcalfe's singing were often lukewarm. The relationship suffered.

In late June 1914, war in Europe seemed inevitable. Casals and his wife stored Casals's papers in a Paris warehouse and rented a house in London. In August, German armies advanced on Belgium. As few as 6 poorly armed Belgian divisions battled 34 divisions of the powerful German war machine, and Casals worried about his friends Eugène Ysaÿe and Queen Elisabeth.

Casals did not learn about Queen Elisabeth's wartime experiences until years later, but in a short time he was relieved to learn that Ysaÿe and his family were safe in London. Bauer was in the United States. Fritz Kreisler had been drafted into the Austrian army and was wounded on the Russian front. As World War I turned Europe into a bloody battleground, Casals and his wife sailed to the United States in November.

New York City had become a haven for refugee musicians, and Casals was welcomed. During 1915 and 1916 he toured with Fritz Kreisler, now recovered from his war wounds, and made headlines everywhere. The critics praised Casals's talents, one calling him "a virtuoso among virtuosos."

Although German submarines infested the waters of the Atlantic, sinking the *Lusitania* in May 1915, Casals and Metcalfe sailed for England en route to Spain that month, returning in the fall for the 1915–16 season. Casals's old friend Enrique Granados was not as fortunate. He was in New York with his wife, Amparo, for the debut of his opera *Goyescas* at the Metropolitan. It was the first grand opera in Spanish, and both men wished that Count de Morphy could have lived to attend the world premiere on January 28, 1916. Granados had planned to leave soon after the premiere, but he was invited to the White House to perform for President Woodrow Wilson. On March 11, Granados and his wife sailed for Barcelona. En route, their ship was torpedoed, and the 48-year-old musician and his wife drowned.

Heartbroken, Casals and Kreisler organized a benefit concert at the Metropolitan Opera House to raise funds for the orphaned Granados children. During intermission, Casals himself stood in the lobby selling Spanish dolls and programs.

Startling news came from Russia a few months later. As Russian soldiers returned from the front, maimed and exhausted, they found their families starving at home while the Russian aristocrats continued to flaunt their wealth in the streets. Demonstrators took to the streets chanting, "Bread and peace!" When soldiers from workers' families joined them, the czar could not stop the momentum of history, and the first socialist revolution was born.

Casals heard that his friend Siloti had fled to Antwerp, Belgium, and he immediately traveled there. The Siloti family had been ordered to share their grandiose home with a group of revolutionaries. Their money had been confiscated. Casals's opinion of the workers' revolution hardened: "[W]hat gives the leaders of revolution the right to think that under the pretext of establishing a new and better social order they can persecute blindly precisely those people who have practiced fraternity with the workers and the people?" Casals gave the Siloti family money to sail to the United States and helped Siloti line up a faculty position at the

Wounded French soldiers parade down the streets of Paris in the aftermath of World War I. When Casals returned to Paris in 1918, he found that the spirit of the city had been ravaged by war. In 1919, he decided to return to and settle in his beloved Catalonia.

Juilliard School of Music in New York City. Years later, when Casals appealed for money for Spanish refugees, Siloti's daughter returned the amount Casals had given her father, with interest.

The United States declared war against Germany in early 1918. New York music circles shunned the works of Beethoven and other German composers. Casals and a few other musicians formed the Beethoven Association of New York to counter the foolishness. By summer, as the war drew to a close, Casals longed to return to Spain, and Metcalfe wanted to stay in her own country. During the summer, the couple traveled to Villa Casals and Metcalfe's attitude hardened. She hated the place, complaining bitterly that the sea air damaged her voice. Casals was dismayed that his favorite place in the world could be so disagreeable to his wife.

When World War I came to a close, Casals returned to Paris and found a bitter, broken city. Bandaged and crippled war veterans wandered the streets. Casals was disappointed to find that the boxes of letters and other mementos he had stored had in his absence been rifled by the police, perhaps because of his open support for Dreyfus years earlier. Most of his treasured letters were gone. Resuming his European tour, Casals was horrified at the sight of the ruined cities and the graves of thousands of young soldiers, especially in Belgium, which had been occupied for four years by the Germans. He hoped that there would never be another war, that he could make the world a little more beautiful with his music.

In 1920, Casals began to pursue his interest in conducting by forming an orchestra in Barcelona. With the help of his brother Enrique, he held auditions and raised the necessary funds, and the first performance of the Orquesta Pau Casals took place on October 13 of that year.

CHAPTER SIX

Sweet Dreams and Nightmares

Casals's marriage had been emotionally dead for years. He was also dissatisfied with having to travel so much. So in the fall of 1919, he decided to settle permanently in Catalonia. The separation from Metcalfe remained unofficial until 1928, but despite occasional joint appearances she and Casals went their separate ways. Just as he refused to discuss his relationship with Suggia in 1912, Casals had only this to say about his failed marriage: "We were . . . ill suited to one another. . . . Our life together was not a happy one. But these . . . are things one does not discuss."

Back in his beloved Catalonia, Casals had a new idea for the future. Cello playing had brought him fame and wealth, but on the few occasions when he had conducted an orchestra, he had been free of anxiety and thrilled by the experience. "If I have been happy scratching away at a cello, how shall I feel when I can possess the greatest of all instruments, the orchestra," he wrote to his composer friend Julius Röntgen.

Neutral throughout World War I, Spain had improved its economy as it supplied iron and raw materials to the warring nations. Barcelona had become a major industrial center, but cultural life for the expanded population of a million and a half people was unimpressive. Casals was convinced that Barcelona deserved its own first-class orchestra. His offers to help improve two existing mediocre orchestras that performed rarely were rejected. The conductors were eager to have Casals appear as a soloist to raise funds, but they insisted that there were not enough capable musicians in the city or adequate public interest to justify a full-time orchestra. Casals disagreed and announced that he was looking for 88 musicians. He would pay twice the going rate for two seasons each year, spring and fall.

Casals's brother Enrique, 27 years old and an accomplished violinist, was enthusiastic about the project. He had returned home two years earlier, when an amnesty was declared for war resisters, and married a local Vendrell woman, María. They had a daughter, Pilar, named after his mother. Agreeing to become the assistant director and first violinist of the new Orquesta Pau Casals, Enrique Casals and his family moved to his brother's house on Diagonal Street. The house also served as the temporary headquarters and social hall for the fledgling orchestra.

Auditions for players were held by Enrique Casals, but it was difficult to find experienced musicians. Thus, many of the people hired were talented amateurs or professionals who had never played with an orchestra. It would be hard work to shape them into a cohesive team. Editorials and letters in opposition to the formation of the orchestra appeared regularly in the press. Wealthy Catalans, fearing low returns on their investments, refused to contribute. Many of them preferred the bullring. Casals asked Queen María Cristina for a grant, but times had changed. Industrial growth had produced a large working class that yearned for democracy. Barcelona was the center of a movement for Catalan independence as well as an anarchist stronghold. Perhaps hoping that the name Pablo Casals would give the monarchy a better image, the

The Belgian violinist Eugène Ysaÿe. To the disappointment of music lovers around the world, Ysaÿe, who had been a great virtuoso in his prime, retired because of illness while only in his fifties. Casals persuaded the violinist to come out of retirement in 1926.

queen offered to finance Casals's orchestra in Madrid. But Casals refused. The capital, he pointed out, already had a symphony orchestra.

During the next seven years, Casals gave more than $300,000 out of his concert fees to finance his dream. The first concert was held on October 13, 1920. Most of Barcelona's wealthy boycotted it. Those who came cheered loudly, but several critics wrote negative reviews. "As a conductor, Casals is a first rate cellist," one commented sarcastically.

But Casals was determined to pull Catalonia out of the musical backwaters of Europe. He refused to perform in public in Barcelona except when he soloed with his orchestra. His point was clear: If people wanted to hear Pablo Casals play the cello, they would have to buy tickets for the Orquesta Pau Casals. Casals also called on many old friends, like Thibaud, Ysaÿe, and Kreisler, to solo with the orchestra. Casals also used the orchestra to provide a debut stage for talented students like cellist Maurice Eisenberg, who had studied with Casals at San Salvador.

The orchestra toured small Catalan cities and towns, charging lower ticket prices to attract workers and peasants to the concerts. Though many of the musicians were skeptical, Casals was confident he could bring common people to the concert halls, remembering the weaver José Anselmo Clavé, who died two years before Casals's birth, and how he was able to form workers' choruses in almost every town in Spain. He also remembered the porter, a proud member of a workers' musical organization, whom he had heard humming Brahms in Vienna.

Casals spoke with union leaders, and by May 1926 the Working-man's Concert Association had been formed. Subscribing members paid affordable fees to attend six Sunday afternoon concerts a year, and the 2,000-seat hall was packed by cheering miners, dockworkers, farmers, and their families. Eventually, the association members organized a music school, an orchestra, and a choral group of its own. They performed in prisons and hospitals. Membership grew from less than 3,000 to 300,000, and the idea of classical music for workers and poor people spread all over Catalonia and even to London.

Meanwhile the Orquesta Pau Casals played to full houses at the Palace of Music. Pilar Casals was sometimes there, sitting proudly and quietly, watching her son conduct. Men who had once mocked the orchestra had nothing but praise for Casals's ability to "give life to composition."

During those years, Casals kept in close contact with his old friends. In late 1926, he traveled to Belgium to visit Eugène Ysaÿe, who, diabetic and arthritic, had retired from the concert stage after a disastrous final concert. Casals was planning a gala concert for the occasion of Beethoven's upcoming centennial, and he urged Ysaÿe to play Beethoven's violin concerto. Ysaÿe said that he was incapable of performing, but Casals insisted. As weeks went by, Casals feared that he had pushed his friend too hard when Ysaÿe's son told him that his father was practicing night and day, learning to play his violin all over again for the coming performance.

Ysaÿe's return to the concert stage was a tremendous success. Faltering at first, the determined violinist quickly recovered and played beautifully. The audience lept to its feet for a lengthy ovation, and later backstage Casals and his old friend embraced and wept with joy. Deeply moved by the evening's events, Ysaÿe sank to his knees and exclaimed, "Resurrection!"

Casals continued to maintain other long-standing friendships. Elisabeth, queen of Belgium, for example, remained Casals's friend for life, and he and Donald Tovey, estranged since the breakup with

Suggia, mended their relationship at two recitals in New York in 1925. The Thibaud-Cortot-Casals trio still toured frequently, and Harold Bauer also played with Casals on some of his tours in the United States.

But events in Spain put a strain on Casals's relationship with Queen María Cristina and Alfonso XIII. On July 21, 1921, the forces of Moroccan independence defeated Spanish colonial forces. In three days, 16,000 Spanish soldiers were killed. The demand for democracy and the abolition of the monarchy swept over Spain. On September 13, 1923, a military coup dissolved the Cortes and placed control of Spain in the hands of a dictator, General Miguel Primo de Rivera, who declared martial law and killed many Liberals. In the mid-1920s, the armies of France and Spain reasserted control over all of Morocco. Alfonso XIII remained a figurehead king of Spain, especially hated in Catalonia for calling himself the heir to the first Bourbon king, Felipe V, who was regarded as the man who had stripped Catalonia of its power. Casals visited Madrid and tried to convince the queen mother and Alfonso that a public apology was in order, but they refused. The king then asked Casals to play his cello at a special concert of Orquesta Pau Casals for Barcelona's International Exposition of 1929. The royal party arrived late to a smattering of polite applause. Then Casals walked on stage. Everyone in the audience rose from their seats, cheering and clapping for the famous cellist. Someone pointed at Casals, shouting, "This is our king," and booed Alfonso. Another demonstrator pointed to the red-faced monarch, yelling, "If he is our king then Pau is our emperor." The police were summoned and the demonstrators were clubbed and arrested. It was several minutes before calm was restored and an embarrassed Casals began to play. Shortly after the incident, Casals saw the king again. Queen María Cristina had died, and after a few minutes of reminiscing, Alfonso remarked, "I'm happy to see how well the Catalans like you, Pablo."

In 1929, Villa Casals was vastly expanded with the addition of a salon, a music hall, and a library. Under Luis Casals's direction, the property was landscaped with terraces, trees, and shrubs. Pablo Casals enjoyed many days at his beautiful beach estate with his mother, brothers, and their wives and children. Often he strolled through Vendrell, chatting with the villagers who all greeted him as "Pau." He expected to live out the rest of his life there, but again history intervened.

The Great Depression of the 1930s swept over the U.S. and Europe, bringing widespread unemployment and hunger. Demonstrators in the streets of Madrid demanded elections, and members of the armed forces marched with them. When two usually opposed groups, the Republicans and the socialists, agreed to work together to establish a democratic republic, Primo de Rivera fled to Paris, and King Alfonso XIII, already in disfavor with the people, now lost the support of the Catholic church. In a desperate move, he agreed to elections to choose between monarchy or a parliamentary form of government, hoping the new coalition would crumble.

Only the anarchists opposed the elections, believing that a republic would continue to support the powerful, greedy landowners and industrialists, doing nothing to improve the lot of workers and peasants. Some anarchists carried out a few bombings and other acts of violence, all of which Casals abhorred. The electorate opted for a republic and on April 12, 1931, when Casals was 53, Pilar Casals's dream of a republic became a reality—but one month too late for her to see it happen. On March 13, on tour in Switzerland, Casals learned that his beloved mother had died.

Pilar Casals was undoubtedly the one person, other than Pablo Casals himself, who did the most for her son's success. With her loving devotion, she had nurtured Pablo's dream of becoming a great musician, and she had guided his career with her practical intelligence. Her belief in his enormous talent never wavered, and thanks mostly to her he was able to bring a wealth of feeling to the world. Once Pablo had become a wealthy, internationally acclaimed virtuoso, he had offered many times to buy her jewelry and other finery, but she always refused. Even though she was a widow, she said that she was still "the wife of a poor man." She was buried beside her husband in the Vendrell cemetery.

Casals celebrated the birth of Spain's Second Republic with the people of Barcelona, dancing and singing in the streets. A few days later the king left for Italy, taking a sizable chunk of the royal treasury with him. In Italy he would be protected by his friend Benito Mussolini.

The new Spanish government was composed of moderates who found it nearly impossible to keep their promises without enraging the wealthy classes and the Church. The peasants demanded land, but the Church intended to retain control over thousands of un-tilled acres. The people wanted free public schools, but the Church was in charge of education; the workers called for living wages, but the owners of the mines and factories refused to grant their demands. Meanwhile the Catalans and Basques were demanding independence. Support for the anarchists increased as people grew pessimistic about the Second Republic.

Casals was torn. On one hand the new government enriched the cultural life of the country and built hospitals and schools, but on the other it sent the hated Civil Guard to shoot down striking workers. When right-wing Conservatives sponsored promonarchy riots, the provisional government countered by scheduling elections for a national Cortes for June 28, 1931. On election day, moderate socialists and progressive Republicans won the majority of the seats in the legislative body and went to work preparing a

Jubilant Spanish railroad workers celebrate the declaration of the Second Spanish Republic on April 12, 1931. The banner mounted on the front of the locomotive reads, Long Live the Republic—Railway Workers of the Northern Railroad.

new constitution that would include many of the rights commonly granted in Western democracies.

However, the new laws were seldom enforced, and as disillusionment grew, a new right-wing bloc uniting the monarchists with other anti-Republican forces gained strength in the Cortes in late 1933. José Antonio Primo de Rivera, son of the now dead dictator, organized the Fascist Falange.

While Spain plummeted into civil strife in the fall of 1934, Casals was awarded an honorary doctorate at the University of Edinburgh, Scotland, where Donald Tovey was a professor of music. Casals conducted Edinburgh's Reid Symphony Orchestra in the first performance of a new cello concerto composed by Tovey, and at the concert he met Albert Schweitzer for the first time. Schweitzer, an internationally recognized medical doctor, humanitarian philosopher, theologian, and philanthropist who had run a hospital in Africa, was also a respected musicologist, specializing in the organ music of Bach. Schweitzer, too, received an honorary degree from Edinburgh that fall. He and Casals felt a closeness immediately and remained friends for decades.

In October 1934, miners organized a strike with the aim of improving working conditions in the Spanish mining region of Asturias, and the government cracked down on the strikers.

Francisco Franco, the veteran general under whose direction a bid for Moroccan independence had been crushed, ordered

A detachment of the Civil Guard fires on Republican supporters in the early 1930s. While Casals was touring the world with his cello, the Second Spanish Republic got off to a troubled start, and by 1934 Spain was tumbling into a state of civil strife.

his forces to open fire on the striking miners. More than 1,000 workers were slaughtered, and another 30,000 were arrested and imprisoned.

Meanwhile, hatred grew for the Republican leaders who had ordered the troops into Catalonia. When Prime Minister Manuel Azaña came to make peace, he was thrown in jail, and Catalans fought in the streets for autonomy. In October 1934 Luis Companys, the leader of the Catalan nationalists, proclaimed a separate Catalan state. Again, martial law was declared and troops moved in, this time killing 29 people. Companys and his entire cabinet were thrown in jail. People began collecting weapons and storing them in attics and cellars.

A noisy and confusing election campaign went on during January 1936. To stave off the growing right-wing threat, prodemocracy Spaniards and Catalans created the Popular Front, an electoral coalition with the goal of defending the Republic. The monarchists and Fascists also united, forming the National Front party. The Popular Front swept the election, and with the flag of the Republic flying overhead the Orquesta Pau Casals played Beethoven's Ninth Symphony to a jammed concert hall.

Again unwilling to play the wait-and-see game, peasants all over Spain carried out their own land reform measures, seizing and redistributing unoccupied lands. In every major industrial center, strikers demanded that promises be kept. Azaña reluctantly suspended rent payments in the countryside and declared the occupied lands the property of the squatters. Thousands of political prisoners were freed, and support for the Republic revived.

Meanwhile, Casals toured the major cities of the world. In Paris he stayed at the home of Maurice and Paula Eisenberg, playing cello and tennis with his host. Honorary degrees, medals, and other prizes regularly came his way during this period in his life. During those first few months of 1936, Casals had high hopes for peace and progress in the world. But then, in July 1936, the shadow of fascism fell over Spain.

Franco's tanks moved into Barcelona after the Fascists took the city in January 1939. Fighting continued around Madrid until March, but then Franco launched a final, all-out offensive. The last remaining Republican garrisons surrendered, and on April 1 the Fascists declared victory.

CHAPTER SEVEN

The Darkest Days

Jubilation over the defeat of the Fascist uprising in 1936 was short-lived. Franco appealed to Mussolini for ships and planes to bring his armies to Spain, and the Italian dictator passed the request on to Hitler, who considered using Spain as a testing ground for new military tactics and bombing techniques. By the end of July and for the next three years, the Germans and Italians sent thousands of troops into Spain and launched ferocious bombing raids on Spanish cities and towns. The Western nations pledged neutrality, while British and U.S. businessmen sold supplies to the Fascists. The British refused to fuel the Republican navy's ships but gladly refueled Hitler's in Gibraltar. The Soviet Union, preparing for a possible Nazi invasion, sent only limited aid to the Spanish pro-democracy forces, called the Loyalists.

The unity of the democratic forces in Spain broke down rapidly. Casals had been delighted by the advances made in autonomous Catalonia. Before the July 18 Fascist uprising, laws on women's rights were enacted, factories were run by the workers, and cultural activities were given the support they needed. Catalonia was attempting to build a model egalitarian society.

However, after the initial July victory against the first Fascist military threat, as soon as their dead friends and relatives were buried, bands of enraged citizens took justice into their own hands. Knowing that most churchmen and landowners had applauded the Fascist insurgents, they burned churches, arrested and executed hundreds of wealthy Barcelonans, and threw open the prison doors. During this chaotic period, innocent people were attacked and, along with thousands of political prisoners, criminals were liberated.

Horrified by the violence, Casals urged Barcelona's public officials to keep order. He also talked to anarchist leaders, who insisted that the people would only fight the Fascists if they had something worth defending. In Madrid, the Republican government and the Communist party disagreed with the anarchists, insisting that reforms be postponed in order to appease the landowners and the Church in the hopes of uniting all Spain against the invaders. While struggling against Franco, the warring pro-democracy factions were soon killing one another.

In August, Franco's troops marched into Seville, bragging that they would take Madrid in a few days. Franco commanded from Seville as truckloads of his men moved north, slaughtering all who tried to defend their towns. In early fall, German planes dropped tons of bombs on Madrid, concentrating on working-class neighborhoods, centers of anti-Fascist opposition. Casals wanted to stay in Catalonia, but his friends persuaded him to tour and use his moral authority to convince the rest of the world to aid the Spanish Republic.

For the next two and a half years, Casals performed in Europe, South America, even North Africa and the Far East, raising funds for food, clothing, and medicine for the war victims. At night he was horrified as he listened to radio reports of the carnage in Spain. Fascists spread rumors that Casals was a Communist, even an anarchist, despite his well-known democratic views. In Switzerland, many of his wealthy fans boycotted his concerts or jeered while he played.

On November 7, 1936, Franco's army reached Madrid, where 15,000 untrained, poorly armed civilians dug trenches around the edge of the city to stop the Fascists. As bombers roared over their heads, they chanted *¡No pasarán!* Then, seemingly out of nowhere, 3,000 volunteers, members of the International Brigades, marched into Madrid to fight on the side of the Loyalists, and democracy was temporarily saved.

When Casals heard the news of Madrid's heroic resistance, his heart overflowed with pride. But he realized that the Spanish people could not hold out without help. On April 26, 1937, Franco's German friends launched a massive bombing campaign

The city of Guernica, the ancient capital of the Basque Republic, was destroyed by German bombers as part of Franco's campaign to capture northern Spain. After the war, Franco made it a crime in Spain to mention the raid, in which more than 1,600 people were killed and nearly 1,000 wounded.

on the small town of Guernica, the ancient capital of the Basque Republic. The bombers filled the skies in the afternoon, when people would be shopping in the town square. More than 1,600 people were dead within minutes, and nearly 1,000 wounded. The horrific scene of slaughter was immortalized by the Spanish artist Pablo Picasso in his masterpiece *Guernica*.

The Basque country was subdued quickly, and Franco turned to Catalonia, the home of his most militant opponents, ordering a similar terror bombing of Barcelona. The only European government protest came from France, where Léon Blum, a democratic socialist, had been elected premier. Blum opened the French frontier, and some supplies arrived, but they were too little and too late. The Soviet Union did nothing, having no desire to help anarchists and socialists who had criticized the brutal regime of Soviet dictator Joseph Stalin.

In March 1938, Hitler occupied Austria. Casals and other supporters of Spanish democracy hoped that now the western nations would intervene. Instead, in the fall, the leaders of Great Britain, France, Germany, and Italy signed the infamous Munich Pact, giving Hitler the green light to invade Czechoslovakia. It was a death blow to the Spanish Republic.

In October 1938, Casals came home to the rubble of Barcelona, so different from the beautiful city where he had first learned to play the cello. The streets were filled with the injured and homeless, wandering with the hollow eyes of the half-dead. Casals scheduled a fundraiser for the war victims, during which he broadcast a fervent plea to the democratic nations of the world: "Do not commit the crime of allowing the murder of the Spanish Republic. If you allow Hitler to win in Spain, you will be the next victims of his madness. The war will spread to . . . the whole world. Come to the aid of the people." His words proved prophetic, but the plea fell on deaf ears.

Casals was at the home of Maurice and Paula Eisenberg in Paris when news of the invasion of Catalonia came over the air waves on

Refugees of the Spanish Civil War file into France in February 1939. With Spain in the hands of the Fascists, some 400,000 Spaniards who had fled Spain for France during the war refused to return home for fear of execution, and Casals began a personal crusade to deprive the Franco regime of international recognition.

December 23, 1938. Thousands of terrified refugees raced for the French border. They were bombed and strafed with machine-gun bullets as they staggered along the road. Casals left for home, despite the urging of his friends that he remain in Paris.

Barcelona was occupied on January 26, 1939. Just two days earlier, Casals had been whisked to the university and presented with a hastily hand-lettered honorary degree in music. Then, just ahead of Franco's forces, Casals left for France. On March 28, 1939, Casals was on tour, playing at a benefit concert for Spanish children in London, when he learned that Madrid had fallen to Franco a few hours earlier. The beasts who wanted to cut off the hands of musicians ruled his homeland.

On his return to Paris, at the Eisenbergs' home, Casals paced the rooms, despairing and ill. He wanted to go home to his family, but everyone warned him he would be executed if he did. Word finally arrived that his brothers had fled to Barcelona and that Villa Casals had been looted by the Fascists.

For weeks Casals could scarcely move from his bed. It was news of others less fortunate than himself that finally shook him out of his breakdown. A refugee acquaintance from Catalonia visited and told him about the hundreds of thousands of his fellow Spaniards and Catalans, packed into temporary camps in France, without adequate water, food, or clothing. Disease swept through the hastily constructed barracks and hundreds died each day. His friend suggested Casals settle in Prades, in the south of France, only 30 miles or so from the Spanish border. While there, Casals could tour France and raise money for the refugees.

Forgetting his own misfortunes, Casals headed south to Prades. Settling into a sparsely furnished room at the Grand Hotel, he soon was hard at work on behalf of Franco's victims in nearby camps. Casals invited Frasquita Capdevila, the loyal secretary of Orquesta Pau Casals and widowed in the late 1920s, to work with him in Prades, and she accepted. Enrique Casals's daughter Pilar also joined her uncle in France. Juan Alavedra, a Catalan poet, managed to escape over the Pyrenees with his wife and two children, and they too became part of the Casals's entourage.

On May 10, 1940, Germany's Nazi "storm troops," as they were known, swept through Belgium, Holland, and Luxembourg and then invaded France from the north. Warned to flee or risk his life, Casals decided to sail to Argentina with his friends. They managed to reach Bordeaux, the roads cramped with thousands of other refugees, only to learn that the boat they were to take had hit a mine and sunk that very morning. There remained one ray of hope when Alavedra met with Casals's old friend Cortot, but clearly the violinist did not wish to antagonize the approaching Germans. He sent his regards to Casals but offered no help, not even temporary shelter for the night.

Cortot continued to play his violin for the pleasure of the occupiers of his homeland all during the war, even accepting a position in the Ministry of Cultural Affairs for the puppet Vichy French government set up by the Nazis. After the war, he came to Casals's doorstep in Prades to confess his shame and ask forgiveness. Because he told the truth, Casals shook his hand, but they never played together again.

Retracing their steps, when Casals's exhausted party arrived at their Prades hotel in the middle of the night, the hotel manager, terrified that the Germans would take reprisals against him, refused to let them in. They were finally offered mattresses on the floor by a tobacco shop owner and a few days later rented a small cottage. The Alavedras and Capdevila lived on the first floor, and Casals climbed a steep flight of outside stairs to a one-room studio. Casals's niece Pilar decided to return home.

Casals continued his fundraising. Truckloads of clothing and food were bought by his earnings to help ease the burden in the refugee camps. He visited several camps in person, comforting the ill and dying, his own energies depleted from insufficient food and exhaustion.

On June 13, 1940, the Germans marched triumphantly into Paris. A few months later they entered Prades. Casals's cottage was searched, and he was put under constant surveillance. When a group of Nazis came to his house and asked him to play his cello, he claimed he no longer played because of rheumatism. They stayed for two hours, one of them toying with Casals's cello, plucking the strings as Casals trembled with rage. For as long as the Nazis were in Prades, Casals did not play. Instead he concentrated on composing music to a lengthy ode to peace by Alavedra, *El Pesebre* (The Manger).

During the winter of 1944, Casals was often ill. There was little to eat except greens, coal was scarce, and the cottage was damp and chilly. Over the radio, which he had hidden from the Nazis, Casals listened to broadcasts from London, which was under nightly bombardment. The United States had entered the war in 1941, after the Japanese joined the Axis Powers in partnership with Germany and Italy and bombed the U.S. Pacific Naval Station at Pearl Harbor, Hawaii. The Soviet Union had been invaded by the Nazis, too, and the Soviet people were engaged in a life-and-death struggle. Rumors were confirmed that the Nazis were exterminating millions of Jews throughout Europe.

In June 1944, news filtered through of the long-awaited Second Front, the landing of American soldiers on the coast of France in Normandy. In December the German occupation forces in Prades were pulled out to serve on the Russian and western fronts. Casals started practicing his cello again.

In May 1945, as Russian soldiers from the east and American soldiers from the west met in Berlin, Europe was liberated. Hitler and Mussolini were dead—the German dictator by his own hand and the Italian hanged in a public square by his own people. Casals believed that now Spain would be freed from the yoke of fascism. But Franco was already making peace with the Allies, offering them the use of Spanish ports and air bases.

Orchestras competed for Casals's first performance since the outbreak of World War II, and Casals chose London. At the age of 68, he flew to England and played with the BBC Orchestra on June 25, 1945, to a packed house of more than 10,000 people.

In August 1945, Japan surrendered after the United States dropped two atomic bombs on the cities of Hiroshima and Nagasaki.

In October, Casals returned to England and heard prominent people speaking favorably about the accomplishments of the Franco regime. "Was it conceivable," he said, "that the Spanish people—the very people who had first taken up arms against fascism—were doomed to continue living under fascist rule?" He addressed the House of Commons and visited a number of prominent people in England, imploring them to use their influence in the interest of democracy in Spain, but the British turned deaf ears to Casals's pleas. Angry and hurt, he rejected offers of honorary degrees from Oxford and Cambridge Universities, announcing that he would defer "until the position of England in respect to Spain is changed." He canceled all future engagements in England, stating that he would never play there as long as any government recognized Franco.

On March 4, 1946, the United States, Britain, and France issued an appeal to the Spanish people to oust the Franco regime. For Casals, it was a cruel and cynical gesture. His fellow countrymen and -women had been crushed and disarmed. The most militant of them were dead or refugees in foreign lands. The only way that Spain could be liberated was through armed intervention by the West. Casals announced that he would turn down offers to perform in any country that recognized the Franco regime. When nothing changed after more than a year, he vowed that he would never play in public *anywhere* or set foot in Spain as long as Franco ruled.

Musicians around the world tried to dissuade Casals from his decision, offering him huge fees. But Casals would not budge, saying only, "Someone must remember." He wrote dozens of letters to statesmen and newspapers and then returned to Prades and a quiet routine—practicing his cello, composing, and teaching. Music students flocked to Prades, seeking to study with the great teacher. Close to Casals's 70th birthday in 1946, a friend arranged a sentimental reunion for the Casals family in a nearby village. The cellist played part of his peace oratorio *El Pesebre* and returned home a little happier.

Despite some of the townspeople referring to Casals as the "hermit of Prades," he was seldom alone. The Alavedra family returned to Barcelona in 1949, but Frasquita Capdevila still managed the household, and there was always at least one visiting relative or friend. One friend, the violinist Alexander Schneider, visited Prades twice, attempting to lure Casals out of retirement. Schneider proposed that the great interpreter of Bach, Casals, give a concert in Prades in 1950 to commemorate the 200th anniversary of Bach's death. Casals agreed, and Schneider returned home to line up an impressive program for the festival.

The 1950 Festival Orchestra was made up of skilled and talented musicians from around the world, including soloists from several prestigious orchestras. People filled the area, and for a few weeks Prades was the music capital of the world. At the festival the Catalan flag flew, and Catalan guests reminded everyone about conditions in their native land. Franco's government passed regulations forbidding Spaniards to travel to Prades, but many Catalans risked their lives crossing the Pyrenees to be there. Casals's dear friend Queen Elisabeth of Belgium came to almost every Prades festival. She had been kept a virtual prisoner in her palace throughout the war and sympathized deeply with Casals's desire to see Spain free again.

Casals opened the festival's first day with a Bach suite. The reviewers were amazed at the 74-year-old musician, still calling him the best cellist in the world and a brilliant conductor. Soon after the festival, Casals started recording with Columbia Records.

Some visiting American soloists urged Casals to write to U.S. president Harry Truman on the issue of Spain. When he did, it was to protest a U.S. loan of $62.5 million to Franco's government at the end of 1950. Less than two months later, the United Nations permitted Spain to participate in UN activities, paving the way for membership.

In 1951, after 17 years, Casals was reunited with Albert Schweitzer in Zurich, at the first performance of the completed oratorio *El Pesebre.* Schweitzer commented that it was better to create than to protest. But Casals responded: "There are times the only creative thing we can do is protest; we must refuse to accept what is evil or

In 1951, Casals was reunited with his old friend the Swiss medical doctor and philanthropist Albert Schweitzer in Zurich, Switzerland, at the first performance of Casals's oratorio El Pesebre. *During the 1950s, the two worked together to slow the arms race between the superpowers.*

wicked." Casals's words apparently influenced Schweitzer to take a stand against nuclear armaments and testing.

Although Casals no longer toured, he traveled to Switzerland every summer to teach cello at the Summer Academy of Music in the Swiss Alps. In May 1955, he went on television as the subject of NBC's "Conversations with Great Men," during which he discussed the world events that deeply disturbed him. One of his concerns was the strained relationship between the United States and the Soviet Union.

During World War II the Soviet Union and United States had been allies against the Nazis, but now the so-called superpowers fought over who would have ideological control of the ruins of Europe. Would there be socialism or capitalism? A barrage of anti-Soviet and anti-American propaganda flowed back and forth, creating what became known as the cold war. Anticommunism became the favorite political pastime in the United States, taking the place of antifascism. Many Americans suspected of Communist affiliations were hounded and fired from their jobs. The men who had joined the Abraham Lincoln Brigade, as the U.S. contingent of the International Brigades was called, to save Spanish democracy were among those persecuted. Meanwhile the United States signed a pact making Spain its ally against "the Communist threat." By 1955 there were U.S. air bases on Spanish soil, built with Franco's permission. Casals feared that he would never see his home again.

Fate intervened. Frasquita Capdevila's health took a turn for the worse in early 1955, and Casals called a priest to her bedside. Though he never had a romantic passion for Capdevila, he knew she had loved him for years, and in a chivalrous act of gratitude during her last days he asked the priest to marry them. He had never divorced Susan Metcalfe, but since their marriage had been a civil ceremony, the Church did not recognize it anyway. Capdevila died a short while later. True to his promise, Casals took her body from Prades to Catalonia, where she had asked to be buried next to Pilar Casals. Casals saw his home for the first time in almost two decades. Wandering through Villa Casals, he gazed sadly at the souvenirs of his life. His family and friends begged him to stay, but he insisted that he would only return when Franco was dead. The next morning he was on his way back to Prades.

Casals had first met Marta Angélica Montañez y Martínez at the Second Prades Festival in 1951, when she was only 14. Her long, dark hair flowing down her back reminded Casals of pictures he had seen of his mother at that age. That year, Montañez returned to Puerto Rico with her uncle, but in 1954 the uncle asked Casals if his niece could study with him.

Marta Montañez arrived in Prades with her mother, and her lessons with Casals began. She had grown into a lovely young woman, self-sufficient, vivacious, mature, and competent. She learned Catalan and assisted Casals with his correspondence. In a short time, Casals was calling her Martita and she addressed him as Uncle Pablo. When summer arrived, it was time for Casals to leave for Switzerland, but he found the idea of leaving Martita hard to bear, and she felt the same way. Casals realized that he had found the love of his life.

Montañez traveled with Casals to Zermatt before visiting Albert Schweitzer; lunching with the exiled American composer and comic genius Charlie Chaplin; spending several days with Queen Elisabeth in Belgium; and walking through Beethoven's birthplace in Bonn, Germany. As fall approached, Enrique and María Casals arrived to join them on Casals's first trip to Puerto Rico, Marta Montañez's home and the birthplace of Casals's mother. As his 80th birthday approached, Casals felt that he was starting his life anew.

In 1957, Casals married his former student Marta Angélica Montañez y Martínez, 61 years his junior, whom he had met at the Second Prade Festival in 1951. Soon after their marriage, the couple settled permanently in her native Puerto Rico.

CHAPTER EIGHT

The Best Years of His Life

In Puerto Rico, Casals immediately felt at home. The sea, the flowers, the mountains of the tropical island delighted him. Everywhere he was greeted with bouquets, serenades, and official banquets. When he was introduced to an audience, he was often described as "one of the three towering figures of the contemporary world"—the others being the socialist physicist Albert Einstein and Casals's friend Albert Schweitzer. The Puerto Rican government provided Casals with a spacious apartment overlooking the ocean.

One day, Casals and Martita went to Mayagüez to see his mother's birthplace. The house in which Pilar Defilló had been born in 1856 turned out to be the very house where Montañez's mother had been born six decades later, both of them, astoundingly, on November 13. The coincidence delighted Casals. A plaque commemorating the birthplace of Casals's mother was placed on the house. People gathered outside and cheered when Casals stepped out onto the balcony with his cello and played the Catalan lullaby his mother had sung to her children.

Casals's energy seemed boundless. In March 1956, after journeying with Montañez to France for the 7th Annual Prades Festival, then on to Switzerland to teach, and to Bonn and Paris for the first Pablo Casals cello competition, he returned to San Juan, Puerto Rico, to prepare for the Festival Casals on April 22, 1957. A week before the festival, Pablo Casals mounted the podium to rehearse the orchestra. It was a very hot day, but Casals had the air conditioning off, preferring what he called "natural air." Suddenly, nausea swept over him, and a severe pain spread across his chest. Calmly, he excused himself and staggered to a dressing room. An ambulance came, but Casals insisted on going home. He knew he was having a heart attack, but what he mumbled to the ambulance attendant was, "What a shame . . . such a wonderful orchestra."

He insisted that the festival go on without him. At the opening concert, the orchestra stood to face an empty podium while Casals's recording of "The Song of the Birds" played to an overflow crowd in the auditorium.

For a month Casals stayed in bed, surrounded by his sister-in-law María Casals, Marta Montañez, and many heart specialists. Later, when he was allowed to sit in a chair, he was still forbidden to play the cello. Afraid that he would never play again if he waited too long, Casals practiced secretly for a few minutes each day until strength began to return to his left hand. "I once more found the music of my cello," he told a happy Marta Montañez.

When Casals was almost his old self again, he and Marta Montañez went ahead with their delayed wedding plans. Their families and friends voiced some opposition because of their age difference, but Casals and Montañez ignored such objections—they knew what they wanted. The matter of a divorce from Susan Metcalfe was handled easily. Casals had not seen her for 30 years, although when she fell ill in Paris in 1951, he had arranged for her care until she was able to go to New Jersey to live with relatives.

Casals and Montañez were married in a civil ceremony on August 3, 1957, and then repeated their vows in a religious ceremony in a San Juan church. Two days later they sailed for Europe, where Casals again taught cello at Zermatt and completed other scheduled activities. They returned to Puerto Rico, having decided to make a permanent home there, and moved into a modest beach house in Santurce, a suburb of San Juan. Casals was happy, sitting under an umbrella on the beach, walking barefoot on the sand with his two dogs, listening to the songs of the waves as he did as a boy at San Salvador.

"I have observed a curious trait in many men," Pablo Casals commented to his biographer. "Though they do not hesitate to say how much they love their mothers, they are reticent to say how much they love their wives! There is no such reticence in me. Martita is the marvel of my world. The years I have shared with Martita have been the happiest years of my life."

Some might have expected Casals, now in his eighties and recovering from a heart attack, to retire and rest on his laurels, but Casals refused to grow old. Asked by an interviewer how he managed to remain so vital and youthful, his answer was simple: "I live! Very few people live!"

In 1957, Casals organized the first Puerto Rican Symphony Orchestra and toured Puerto Rico. He was so active that the press had trouble keeping up with him. For part of each summer, he was

Casals poses with his longtime friend and the founder of the Marlboro Music Festival, the pianist Rudolf Serkin (left), and the festival manager, Anthony Checchia, in Marlboro, Vermont, during the late 1950s. The cellist spent part of several summers in residence playing and teaching at Marlboro.

in Marlboro, Vermont, where his friend and internationally acclaimed pianist Rudolf Serkin had organized a new music festival.
Teaching and conducting at Marlboro was a joy for Casals: He loved
the rustic atmosphere of the town, the beautiful climate, the hills
and streams, the spirit of cooperation among the young musicians
there. He and his wife ate with the students in a converted barn, on
plank tables covered with checkered cloths. In the evening he took
part in informal music making. Queen Elisabeth also visited Casals
in Vermont.

   As the cold war intensified during the 1950s, the United States
and the Soviet Union each worked to attain superiority over the
other with respect to nuclear weapons. These weapons had such
destructive potential that before long both superpowers had the
ability to wipe out the entire world population many times over.
Still the arms race continued unabated. Fearing for their lives,
Americans built home air raid shelters and stocked them with
canned goods, and schools conducted air raid drills in which children were instructed on how to take cover in the event of an air
attack. Of course no bomb shelters or air raid drills could have
warded off the devastation of an actual nuclear war.

   In 1958, Casals and Schweitzer headed the list of notable
people appealing for an end to the arms race and a ban on all
nuclear tests. In an effort to stimulate a wider peace movement,

*Casals performs his own
composition,* Hymn to the
United Nations, *at the UN
in 1971. The piece, with an
accompanying text by the
English poet W. H. Auden,
was commissioned by UN
secretary-general U Thant to
mark the 26th anniversary
of the organization.*

Casals agreed to play at the festivities commemorating the 18th anniversary of the United Nations. The October 24 concert was televised and broadcast to 74 nations. Casals played Bach's Sonata in D Major for cello and piano with his old friend Mieczyslaw Horszowski on piano. When he played his symbolic "Song of the Birds," his homage to Spanish exiles, the audience rose to give him a standing ovation. Fritz Kreisler, by then 83 years old and nearly blind, rushed to the podium and embraced his old friend.

Some people thought that Casals's UN performance would be the climax to his career, but his schedule throughout the 1960s was dizzying, and the press could barely keep up with him. One day there would be a report of his work at the Second Festival Casals in San Juan. Then he would turn up at the Prades Festival. In the spring of 1960, he was teaching cello at the University of California at Berkeley. National Educational Television filmed the event, making a permanent record of his amazing skill as a teacher.

Casals never allowed the press to forget Spain. In 1959, when U.S. president Dwight Eisenhower toured Europe, Casals looked in disgust at newspaper photos showing the smiling president and Franco, the vile dictator of Spain, locked in a farewell hug, and

Casals and the German-born violinist Alexander "Sasha" Schneider stroll through the village of Le Beaux, France, where together they gave an outdoor concert during the late 1950s.

Casals meets with U.S. president John F. Kennedy in the East Room of the White House, in Washington, D.C., in November 1961, after playing for the president, his wife, and their guests. During their meeting, Kennedy told Casals that he would do all he could to bring about world peace.

he immediately made statements condemning the "romance." In 1961, when a recreation center for Spanish refugees, Foyer Pablo Casals, opened in the south of France, Casals again reminded the world that his homeland was in bondage. In the summer and fall of that same year he was in Japan and then in Israel, judging cellists again, returning by way of the United States to play at the White House for the second time in his life. When John F. Kennedy had been elected to the White House, Casals had written to him about Spain, just as he had written to every U.S. president. And this time he received a personal note inviting him to play at the White House.

On November 13, 1961, 60 years after Casals played for President Theodore Roosevelt, Schneider and Horszowski joined him to play for 150 prominent guests in the East Room of the White House. In conversation with Casals after the concert, Kennedy promised to do everything he could to bring peace to the world. Casals believed that Kennedy was sincere.

Early in 1962, Casals toured and performed *El Pesebre* to inspire the fledgling world peace movement. Since he could not transport an entire chorus, he trained singers in every country to perform his work in Catalan. Marta Casals joined the tour. The peace crusade began in San Francisco and went on to North and South America and every corner of Europe. In 1963, the second year of the peace tour, Casals, now in his late eighties, conducted the uncut version of Bach's *Saint Matthew Passion* at Carnegie Hall in New York City. The concert ran for six hours, with a dinner break.

In October, Casals returned to the UN. Five years had gone by since his first concert there, but the prospect for peace and stability in the world seemed a long way off. The nuclear arms race continued, and an escalating civil war in the tiny Southeast Asian country of Vietnam threatened to engage the superpowers. At his second concert at the UN, Casals said to his audience, "How I wish there could be a tremendous movement of protest in all countries . . . to prevent this catastrophe."

A few weeks later Casals was informed that he would be awarded the prestigious Presidential Medal of Freedom for his work to bring about world peace. President Kennedy was to present Casals with the award in Washington, D.C., but on November 22, the president was assassinated in Dallas, Texas. "What monstrous madness!" a horrified Casals said when he heard the news. "Had he not died," Casals commented a few years later, "how many of those who perished in . . . Vietnam might also be alive?"

When Richard Nixon became president in 1968, Casals sent his customary letter on the situation in Spain, which continued to struggle under the Franco's oppressive regime. A Catalan friend sent Casals clippings every week so that he could keep abreast of developments in his homeland. As honorary chairman of Spanish Refugee Aid, Casals continued to assist exiled Spaniards and their children, many of them still living in shantytowns in southern France. "These men and women are owed a debt that alas can never be repaid," Casals told a reporter. "Many people have forgotten what happened in Spain. Freedom will come, but, sadly, I may not live to see it." In response to his letter to Nixon, Casals received only a brief note from a presidential aide.

On April 17, 1970, a Salud Casals (Salute to Casals) took place at Lincoln Center for the Performing Arts in New York City. Casals's own *La Sardana*, a cello piece written in eight-part harmony, climaxed the evening. Seventy cellists from around the world, including 30 of his former students, played under the baton of the 94-year-old Casals. A *New York Times* music critic commented that Casals seemed frail but "at times he did everything but fly off the podium." Reviewers gasped: "Astounding!"

The following year, Casals was in New York conducting the world premiere of his *Hymn to the United Nations*, a setting of a poem by the British writer W. H. Auden. In the spring of 1972, Casals gave five concerts in Venezuela before conducting the *Hymn to the United Nations* at the dedication of the Pablo Casals Cello Library at Arizona State University in Phoenix, Arizona. Only inclement weather prevented him from taking a helicopter tour over the Grand Canyon. Then, in the fall, Casals performed Beethoven's Triple Concerto on his cello in Guadalajara, Mexico, to help raise funds for an orphanage. His last trip abroad was to Israel in the summer of 1973, at age 96. The violinist Isaac Stern met him at the airport. Casals was exhausted from the journey but seemed to recover fully as soon as Stern brought him indoors to play the piano.

Home in Puerto Rico in September 1973, Casals suffered his second heart attack while playing dominoes at a friend's house. In the hospital, Casals pulled the intravenous tubes out and told the nurses, "Damn it, I will not die!" He survived until October 22, 1973.

At requiem services at a church in San Juan the next day, the "Song of the Birds" was played. Casals was buried in a small cemetery fronting on his beloved sea.

On November 20, 1975, just a little more than two years after Casals's death, Franco died. The United States sent Vice-President Nelson Rockefeller to the funeral, but none of the other Western nations sent anyone of rank. Former president Nixon commented

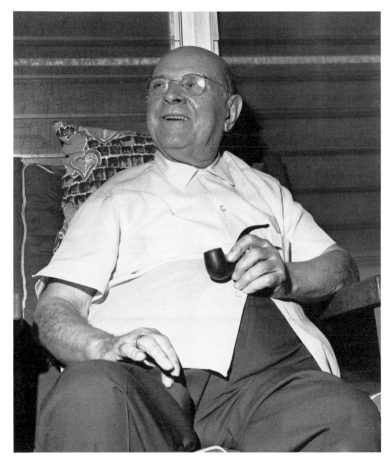

One of the great musicians of the 20th century, Pablo Casals was also a man of deep political conviction and bold action in the struggle for freedom, justice, democracy, and human rights. In his long life, he always held himself to the highest standards, not only as an artist but as a human being.

that Franco had earned respect for Spain through "firmness and fairness," a telling endorsement from a man who had so betrayed the public trust that he had been forced to resign the presidency in shame the previous year.

In 1978, popular demonstrations led to the first free elections in Spain in 41 years, and Spain once more became a constitutional republic. The new republic was declared on December 29, Casals's birthday, a coincidence that would have delighted the world's greatest cellist.

Chronology

1876	Born Pablo Carlos Salvador Casals y Defilló in Vendrell, Catalonia, Spain, on December 29
1880–87	Begins taking piano lessons with father; impressed by the cellist José García, whom he hears in concert
1888	Studies cello with García at Barcelona's Municipal School of Music
1889–91	Plays in Barcelona cafés; the composer Isaac Albéniz gives him letter of introduction to Count de Morphy, adviser to Queen María Cristina in Madrid
1891	Casals's first solo concert
1892	Begins study of Bach's *Suites for Cello Unaccompanied*
1893	Graduates with honors; plays for the queen in Madrid and receives a royal grant
1893–95	Attends Madrid Conservatory of Music and receives general education from Count de Morphy
1895	Loses royal grant by refusing to attend conservatory of music in Brussels; plays in theater orchestra of Folies-Marigny, Paris

1896	Returns to Barcelona; appointed to faculty of Municipal School of Music and teaches privately as well; pays bribe to avoid military service
1897	Organizes trio with Enrique Granados and Mathieu Crickboom; plays at Portugal's Royal Palace; solos with Madrid Symphony Orchestra; awarded Order of Carlos III
1899	Debuts at London's Crystal Palace; plays for England's Queen Victoria; solos with Lamoureux Orchestra
1900–1919	Tours Spain and the Netherlands with the pianist Harold Bauer
1901–4	First U.S. tour, with the singer Emma Nevada, in 1901; returns to Catalonia the following year and gives his first performance of the Bach suites; tours South America with Bauer in 1903; tours the United States and plays at the White House for President Theodore Roosevelt in 1904; second U.S. tour with Bauer
1905–14	World tours as soloist and with the violinists Fritz Kreisler and Eugène Ysaÿe
1906	Forms trio with Thibaud and Cortot, a union that lasts until 1937; they establish a music school in Paris; Casals begins relationship with the Portuguese cellist Guilhermina Suggia
1910	Plays for first time in Vienna
1912	Separates from Suggia

1914	Marries Susan Metcalfe; outbreak of World War I
1915	Casals makes U.S. tour with Fritz Kreisler; Enrique Granados dies, and Casals organizes benefit for his children
1918	United States declares war on Germany; Casals organizes Beethoven Association of New York; plays in Mexico City and is confronted by Mexican revolutionaries
1919	End of World War I; Casals returns to Barcelona, tours war-torn Europe; organizes Orquesta Pau Casals in Barcelona with violinist brother
1920–36	Conducts Orquesta Pau Casals in Europe and United States
1926	Founds Workingman's Concert Association; brings the violinist Eugène Ysaÿe out of retirement to perform at Beethoven Centennial
1931	Celebrates birth of Spain's Second Republic by conducting Beethoven's Ninth Symphony
1933	Nazis take power in Germany; Casals refuses to play there or in Fascist Italy
1934	Awarded an honorary doctorate at the University of Edinburgh, Scotland; meets the philanthropist Albert Schweitzer
1936	Boycotts Berlin Olympics and rehearses his orchestra for alternative festivitics; outbreak of Spanish Civil War; conducts last concert of Orquesta Pau Casals

1936–39	As war rages in Spain, Casals tours Europe, South America, North Africa, and the Far East raising funds for war victims
1937	Germans bomb Guernica and Barcelona
1938	Nazis occupy Austria and Czechoslovakia, unopposed by Western nations; Casals conducts concert in Barcelona and broadcasts appeal to the West for aid for the war victims
1939	Fascist dictator Francisco Franco is victorious in Spain; Casals suffers severe depression in Paris and settles in Prades, France; tours unoccupied zone of southern France and Switzerland to raise money for Spanish refugees; organizes relief effort for Spanish exiles
1939–45	World War II; Casals lives under Nazi occupation of France, refuses to play cello for Nazis; composes peace oratorio with Alavedra's poem *El Pesebre*
1945	End of World War II
1945–50	While living in Prades, Casals continues humanitarian work and protests Franco's dictatorship; bicentenary celebration of Bach's birth in 1950; the violinist Alexander Schneider organizes Bach Festival in Prades and Casals serves as artistic director
1955	Casals appears on television program "Conversations with Great Men;" marries Frasquita Capdevila; begins relationship with Marta Angélica Montañez; U.S. government formally recognizes Franco regime; Casals continues anti-Franco letter-writing campaign

1956   Performs in Veracruz, Mexico; settles in Puerto
                    Rico

1957   First Festival Casals in honor of his 80th birthday;
                    Casals suffers heart attack during rehearsals;
                    organizes Puerto Rico Symphony Orchestra and
                    music conservatory; with Albert Schweitzer, calls
                    for end of arms race; divorces Susan Metcalfe and
                    marries Marta Montañez

1958   Performs at 13th anniversary celebration of UN

1959   U.S. president Dwight Eisenhower tours Spain and
                    embraces Franco

1960   National Educational Television produces films of
                    Casals teaching master classes at the University of
                    California at Berkeley; world premiere of his
                    oratorio *El Pesebre*; Casals judges cellists in Israel
                    and Japan

1961   Plays at White House for President John Kennedy
                    and urges him to break with Franco; teaches and
                    conducts at Vermont's Marlboro Music Festival;
                    Foyer Pablo Casals, recreation center for Spanish
                    refugees, opens in the South of France

1962–63   Casals conducts *El Pesebre* during tour for world
                    peace

1963   Kennedy assassinated; Casals conducts uncut
                    version of Bach's *Saint Matthew Passion* at Carnegie
                    Hall, in New York

1970   Concert honoring Casals at Lincoln Center for the
                    Performing Arts, in New York; Casals conducts 70
                    cellists, including 30 of his former students, in a
                    performance of his *La Sardana*

1971	Conducts world premiere of his *Hymn to the United Nations* at the UN
1972	Gives five concerts in Venezuela and plays at the dedication of the Pablo Casals Cello Library in Phoenix, Arizona; appears in Guadalajara, Mexico, to benefit an orphanage
1973	Attends music festival in Israel; returns to Puerto Rico for Festival Casals; suffers heart attack; dies on October 22
1975–76	Franco dies on November 20, 1975; republic declared in Spain in 1978 on December 29, Casals's birthday

Further Reading

Alavedra, Juan. *Pablo Casals: Biografía.* Barcelona: Plaza and Janes, 1963.

Brome, Vincent. *The International Brigades.* New York: Morrow, 1966.

Casals, Pablo. *Joys and Sorrows: Reflections.* New York: Simon & Schuster, 1970.

Corredor, J. M. *Conversations with Casals.* New York: Dutton, 1956.

Cowling, Elizabeth. *The Cello.* New York: Scribners, 1975.

Feis, Herbert. *The Spanish Story: Franco and the Nations at War.* New York: Knopf, 1948.

Forsee, Aylesa. *Pablo Casals: Cellist for Freedom.* New York: Macmillan, 1965.

Garza, Hedda. *Francisco Franco.* New York: Chelsea House, 1987.

Goldston, Robert. *The Civil War in Spain.* New York: Bobbs-Merrill, 1966.

Hooper, John. *The Spaniards: A Portrait of the New Spain.* New York: Viking Penguin, 1986.

Jackson, Gabriel. *A Concise History of the Spanish Civil War.* New York: John Day, 1974.

Kirk, H. L. *Pablo Casals.* New York: Holt, Rinehart & Winston, 1974.

Landis, Arthur H. *The Abraham Lincoln Brigade.* New York: Citadel Press, 1967.

Payne, Robert, ed. *The Civil War in Spain, 1936–39.* New York: Putnam's 1962.

Taper, Bernard. *Cellist in Exile.* New York: McGraw-Hill, 1962.

Thomas , Hugh. *The Spanish Civil War.* New York: Harper & Brothers, 1961.

Yglesias, José. *The Franco Years.* New York: Bobbs-Merrill, 1977.

Index

Abraham Lincoln Brigade, 88

Academia de Bellas Artes de San Fernando, 19

Alavedra, Juan, 82, 83, 85

Albéniz, Isaac, 38, 41, 43

Alfonso XII, king of Spain, 30, 46, 57, 71, 72

Amelia, queen of Portugal, 50

Army of Africa, 22

Auden, W. H., 98

Azaña, Manuel (prime minister of Spain), 17, 75

Bach, Johann Sebastian, 39, 40, 57, 60, 74

Barcelona, Spain, 15, 19, 20, 23, 25, 26, 27, 28, 30, 32, 33, 35, 37, 39, 40, 48, 50, 64, 68, 69, 73, 80, 82

Barcelona Olympiad, 17

Barcelona's International Exposition of 1929, 71

Bauer, Harold, 54, 55, 57, 62, 63

BBC Orchestra, 84

Beethoven, Ludwig van, 15, 19, 61, 65, 98

Beethoven Association of New York, 65

Beethoven Gold Medal of the Philharmonic Society of London, 62

Blum, Léon, 80

Boixados, Benet, 36

Boixados, María, 36

Brahms, Johannes, 57, 62

Cambridge University, 85

Capdevila, Frasquita, 82, 83, 85, 88

Carlos I, king of Portugal, 50

Carlos, Don, 27

Casals, Arturo (brother), 31

Casals, Carlos (father), 25, 26, 29, 30, 31, 32, 33, 37, 38, 39, 40, 41, 46, 48, 58, 61

Casals, Enrique (brother), 40, 44, 58, 62, 68, 82, 89

Casals, Luis (brother), 38, 40, 44, 58, 62, 71

Casals, Pablo
  birth, 25
  childhood, 30–33
  death, 98
  debuts in London, 50
  first solo concert, 38–39
  marriage, 63, 88, 92
  opens school, 60
  plays in Royal Palace, 44
  receives medals, 46, 50, 62, 97
  receives honorary degree, 74
  records music, 86
  rejects honorary degrees, 85
  studies cello, 36–37, 38
  studies with count, 44–45
  tours United States, 55–57

Casals, Pilar (mother), 25, 28, 29–30, 31, 32, 33, 36, 37, 38, 40, 41, 44, 46, 47, 48, 58, 62, 70, 72–73, 88, 91

Casals, Pilar (niece), 82

Catalonia, 19, 23, 25, 26, 27, 48, 53, 67, 75, 78, 80

Chaplin, Charlie, 89

Clavé, José Anselmo, 69

Columbia Records, 86

Companys, Luis, 75

Concerto in D Minor (Lalo), 50, 51

"Conversations with Great Men," 87

Cortot, Alfred, 59, 60, 82–83

Crickboom, Mathieu, 49

Cristina, María, queen of Spain, 27, 38, 43, 46, 49–50, 57, 68, 69, 71

Defilló, José, 28, 29

Defilló, Raimunda, 28, 29

Dreyfus, Alfred, 54, 55, 65

École Normale de Musique, 60

Einstein, Albert, 91

Eisenberg, Maurice, 69, 75, 80

Eisenberg, Paula, 75, 89

Eisenhower, Dwight, 95

Elisabeth, queen of Belgium, 58, 63, 70, 86, 89, 94

El Pesebre (Alavedra), 83, 85, 86, 96

Falangists, 17, 74

Felip, Francisca, 29, 30

Ferdinand, king of Spain, 27

Ferdinand VII, king of Spain, 27

Festival Casals, 92

First Carlist War, 27–28

Four Insurgent Generals, 17, 22. *See also* Nationalists

Foyer Pablo Casals, 96

Franco, Francisco, 17, 22, 23, 74–75, 78, 79, 81, 84, 85, 86, 88, 95, 97, 98, 99

García, José, 33, 36–37, 39, 49

Gassol, Ventura, 20

Gevaërt, François, 46

Goded, Manuel, 20, 21, 22

Granados, Enrique, 49, 64

Hitler, Adolf, 16, 17, 22, 77, 80, 84

Horszowski, Mieczyslaw, 95, 96

Hymn to the United Nations, 98

Infanta Isabel, 43, 45

International Brigades, 23, 79, 88

Isabel, queen of Spain, 27

Isabella, queen of Spain, 27, 28, 30

Jacobs, Edouard, 46, 47

Juilliard School of Music, 65

Kennedy, John, 96, 97

Kreisler, Fritz, 62, 63, 64, 69

Lalo, Édouard, 50, 51

Lamoureux, Charles, 50–51, 53

La Sardana, 98

Liberalism, 27

Los Tres Bemoles, 32

Madrid, Spain, 19, 21, 22, 38, 41, 47, 50, 51, 54, 69, 71, 72, 78, 79, 81

Madrid Conservatory of Music, 45

Madrid Symphony Orchestra, 50

Marchesi, Mathilde, 54

Martínez, Marta Angélica Montañez y, 88–89, 92, 93

Medal of the Order of Isabel la Católica, 46

Ménard-Dorian, Aline, 54

Ménard-Dorian, Paul, 54

Metcalf, Susan (wife), 63, 64, 65, 67, 88, 92

Metropolitan Opera House, 64

Mola, Emilio, 22

Monasterio, Jesús de, 45–46

Moór, Emanuel, 59–60

Moreau, León, 56

Morphy, Guillermo de, 38, 41, 43, 45, 47, 49, 50, 51, 64

Munich Pact, 80

Municipal School of Music, 33, 49

Mussolini, Benito, 16–17, 22, 73, 77, 84

Nationalists, 17, 21

Nevada, Emma, 50, 55

1950 Festival Orchestra, 86

Ninth Symphony (Beethoven), 15, 17, 75

Nixon, Richard, 97, 98–99

"Ode to Joy," (Schiller), 15

Olympics (1936), 17

Order of Carlos III, 50

Orfeo Catalan Palace of Music, 15, 17, 70

Orquesta Pau Casals, 15, 17, 68–69, 70, 75, 82

Oxford University, 85

Pablo Casals Cello Library, 98

Palace of Montjuich, 15

Pasteur, Louis, 32

Philharmonic of Madrid, 19

Picasso, Pablo, 80

Picquart, Georges, 54–55

Plaza de Cataluña, 35, 40, 49

Popper, David, 60

Popular Front, 17

Presidential Medal of Freedom, 97

Puerto Rican Symphony Orchestra, 93

Queipo de Llano, Gonzalo, 17

Ram, Matilda, 54

Reid Symphony Orchestra

Rivera, José Antonio Primo de, 74

Rivera, Miguel Primo de, 71, 72

Rockefeller, Nelson, 98

Röntgen, Julius, 57–58, 67

Roosevelt, Theodore, 57, 96

Rosanoff, Lieff, 60

Saint Matthew Passion (Bach), 97

Saint-Saëns, Camille, 40, 50, 60

Sanjurjo, José, 22

San Salvador, Spain, 17, 21, 26, 31, 58, 93

Schiller, Friedrich von, 15

Schweitzer, Albert, 74, 86–87, 89, 91, 94

Serkin, Rudolf, 94

7th Annual Prades Festival, 92

Seville, Spain, 17–18

Siloti, Alexander, 58, 64–65

Stalin, Joseph, 80

Stern, Isaac, 98

Suggia, Augusto, 60

Suggia, Guilhermina, 60, 61, 62–63, 67, 71

Suites for Cello Unaccompanied (Bach), 39–40, 57

Summer Academy of Music, 87

Symphony Orchestra of Madrid, 19

Thibaud, Jacques, 59, 60, 69

Tovey, Donald Francis, 62, 70–71, 74

Triple Concerto (Beethoven), 98

Truman, Harry, 86

United Nations, 86, 95

United States, 16, 53, 55–57, 63, 64, 65

University of Edinburgh, 74

Vendrell, Spain, 23, 25, 26, 28, 29, 30, 32, 33, 36, 37, 38, 48, 58, 61, 72

Victoria, queen of England, 50

Villa Casals, 62, 65, 72, 82, 88

Walker, Ernest, 51

Wilson, Woodrow, 64

Workingman's Concert Association, 70

World War I, 63, 65, 68

World War II, 84, 87

Ysaÿe, Eugène, 58, 62, 63, 69, 70

Zola, Émile, 55

PICTURE CREDITS

HEDDA GARZA is a freelance writer and lecturer living in upstate New York. Her articles on little-known Mexican and U.S. history have appeared in several national magazines and newspapers, and her *Watergate Investigation Index* won the *Choice* magazine Best Academic Book Award. She is also the author of *Joan Baez* and *Frida Kahlo* in the Chelsea House series HISPANICS OF ACHIEVEMENT and of four young adult biographies in the Chelsea House series WORLD LEADERS—PAST & PRESENT.

RODOLFO CARDONA is professor of Spanish and comparative literature at Boston University. A renowned scholar, he has written many works of criticism, including *Ramón, a Study of Gómez de la Serna and His Works* and *Visión del esperpento: Teoría y práctica del esperpento en Valle-Inclán.* Born in San José, Costa Rica, he earned his B.A. and M.A. from Louisiana State University and received a Ph.D. from the University of Washington. He has taught at Case Western Reserve University, the University of Pittsburgh, the University of Texas at Austin, the University of New Mexico, and Harvard University.

JAMES COCKCROFT is currently a visiting professor of Latin American and Caribbean studies at the State University of New York at Albany. A three-time Fulbright scholar, he earned a Ph.D. from Stanford University and has taught at the University of Massachusetts, the University of Vermont, and the University of Connecticut. He is the author or coauthor of numerous books on Latin American subjects, including *Neighbors in Turmoil: Latin America, The Hispanic Experience in the United States: Contemporary Issues and Perspectives,* and *Outlaws in the Promised Land: Mexican Immigrant Workers and America's Future.*